Prayer
GUIDE

PRAYERS FROM THE BOOKS OF THE BIBLE

AUGUSTINA AGHANWA-FAKIYESI

BALBOA.
PRESS

A DIVISION OF HAY HOUSE.

Scripture taken from the New King James Version®. Copyright © 1982 by Thomas Nelson. Used by permission. All rights reserved.

Scripture taken from the King James Version of the Bible.

Balboa Press books may be ordered through booksellers or by contacting:

Balboa Press
A Division of Hay House
1663 Liberty Drive
Bloomington, IN 47403
www.balboapress.com
1 (877) 407-4847

Because of the dynamic nature of the Internet, any web addresses or links contained in this book may have changed since publication and may no longer be valid. The views expressed in this work are solely those of the author and do not necessarily reflect the views of the publisher, and the publisher hereby disclaims any responsibility for them.

The author of this book does not dispense medical advice or prescribe the use of any technique as a form of treatment for physical, emotional, or medical problems without the advice of a physician, either directly or indirectly. The intent of the author is only to offer information of a general nature to help you in your quest for emotional and spiritual well-being. In the event you use any of the information in this book for yourself, which is your constitutional right, the author and the publisher assume no responsibility for your actions.

Any people depicted in stock imagery provided by Thinkstock are models, and such images are being used for illustrative purposes only. Certain stock imagery © Thinkstock.

Print information available on the last page.

ISBN: 978-1-5043-7292-3 (sc)
ISBN: 978-1-5043-7293-0 (e)

Balboa Press rev. date: 02/15/2017

Contents

Abstract

This prayer book is the result of a challenge that I gave myself to read from Genesis to Revelation twice in one year. Usually, I read the whole of the bible once in a year, and in the year 2009, I was lazy with studying the bible and I decided to discipline myself by reading through the bible twice in one year instead of once. Out of this challenge came the revelation for the prayer points that are found in this book. The prayer points cover from Genesis to Revelation. This book can help you pray using the word of God as it is written in the Bible. After reading chapters from the bible, this book has some prayer points that are from those chapters. Every book in the bible is covered in this book, but not every chapter is covered. This book is just a guide on how to pray using the WORD. You are encouraged to personalize your prayer points and also pray as the spirit leads you to.

Dedication

This book is dedicated to all believers who want to pray using the bible as a point of reference. To my beloved children who are the gift of God in my life. To my parents who inculcated in me the importance of praying in my early years of life. To my late father – Pa James Aghanwa, who prayed everyday of his life for me and my siblings, making mention of our names daily during prayer and asking our guardian angel to watch over us and protect us daily. To all the ministers of God who have made positive impact in my Christian life.

Genesis

Genesis Chapter 1

The Bible says in Genesis 1: 1 – 2, 28 – In the beginning God created the heaven and the earth. 2 – And the earth was without form, and void; and darkness was upon the face of the deep. And the spirit of God moved upon the face of the waters. 28 - Then God blessed them, and God said to them, "Be fruitful and multiply; fill the earth and subdue it; have dominion over the fish of the sea, over the birds of the air, and over every living thing that moves on the earth." [(New King James Version)(NKJV).

Prayer points:
1. Father, everything in my life that is without form and void, let your spirit begin to move over them in Jesus name
2. Father, my marriage that is without form and void, let your spirit begin to move over it in Jesus name.
3. My home that is without form and void, let your spirit begin to move over it in Jesus name.
4. Let your spirit move over my marriage that is covered with darkness in Jesus name
5. Let your spirit begin to move over my business that is covered with darkness
6. Let your spirit begin to move over my health that is covered with darkness
7. Everything concerning me that is covered with darkness let your spirit begin to move over them in Jesus name.

8. Let your spirit begin to move over my family that is covered with darkness in Jesus name.
9. Every cloud in my business I command you to clear in the name of Jesus.
10. Every cloud in my marriage I command you to clear in the name of Jesus even as the spirit of God begins to move over my marriage in Jesus name.
11. God change my record in Jesus name.
12. God change my failure to success in Jesus name
13. God let my success be great in Jesus name
14. Let me be moved by faith in Jesus name. Amen
15. Devil, you cannot deny me of my possession in Jesus name
16. God change my fear to faith in Jesus name
17. God change my low level to high level in Jesus name
18. Let there be a manifestation of the great intervention of God in my life/home/marriage/education/career/health in Jesus name
19. I am blessed in Jesus name.
20. My home is blessed in Jesus name
21. My marriage is blessed in Jesus name
22. My parents are blessed in Jesus name
23. My children are blessed in Jesus name
24. My labor is blessed in Jesus name
25. Every darkness in the life of my husband/wife disappear in Jesus name.
26. Father, in accordance to your word, may I be fruitful in Jesus name.
27. Father, may I multiply in all that I do, that your word will be made manifest in my life in Jesus name.
28. Father, may I fill the earth with good works, with love by your power and grace in Jesus name.
29. Father, I declare in accordance to your word that I will have dominion over every living thing that moves on the earth in Jesus name. Amen.

30. By the authority the Father has given me, whatever I bind on earth is bound in heaven. Therefore I bind darkness in my home in Jesus name
31. I bind the spirit of division in Jesus name
32. I bind the spirit of hatred in Jesus name
33. I bind the spirit of fear in Jesus name
34. I bind the spirit of war in Jesus name
35. I bind the spirit of the strange woman/man in Jesus name
36. By the authority my Father in heaven has given me that whatever I loose on earth is loosed in heaven, therefore I loose the spirit of love in my home
37. I loose the spirit of unity in my home
38. I loose the spirit of Christ in my home

Genesis Chapter 2

Genesis 2: 24 – Therefore a man shall leave his father and his mother and be joined to his wife, and they shall become one flesh. (NKJV)

Prayer points:
1. Father, teach our men to obey your commandment to leave their father and mother and be joined to their individual wives in Jesus name.
2. Father I pray that the man and the woman that are married shall become one flesh in Jesus name.
3. I take authority over the spirit of the strange woman in our homes
4. I take authority over the spirit of the strange man in our homes
5. I take authority over the spirit of meddling mother in-laws in our homes
6. I take authority over the spirit of meddling friends in our homes
7. May our homes be too hot for enemies in sheep's clothing
8. May our homes be too unconfortable for home wreckers

Genesis Chapter 3

Prayer points:
1. I come against the spirit of idleness
2. I will not entertain the enemy
3. I close every crack in my wall so the serpent will not come in and bite
4. I will not believe the evil report of the enemy
5. Whatever the word of God says, I believe
6. Whatever God says I receive with thanksgiving
7. I come against the lust of the eye
8. I come against the lust of the flesh
9. I come against the pride of life
10. I will take responsibility for my actions and repent of my sins
11. I will not blame another for my mistakes
12. I will identify with the sins of brethren and ask for mercy

Genesis Chapter 4

Genesis 4:7 – "If you do well, will you not be accepted? And if you do not well, sin lies at the door. And its desire is for you, but you should rule over it." (NKJV)

Prayer points:
1. Father I pray that by the power in the blood of Jesus, I will do well that I may be accepted in Jesus name.
2. Every power that will cause me not to do well, I bind you in the name of Jesus.
3. May I not be overcome by sin, may sin not control my life
4. May I have victory over every temptation, every trial and every evil in Jesus name. Amen.

Genesis Chapter 5

Genesis 5: 24 – And Enoch walked with God; and he was not, for God took him. (NKJV)

Prayer points:
1. Father God, like Enoch, give me the grace to walk with you blamelessly in Jesus name. Amen.
2. May I live an exemplary Christian life in Jesus name. Amen.

Genesis Chapter 6

Genesis 6: 3 – And the Lord said, "My Spirit shall not strive with man forever, for he is indeed flesh; yet his days shall be one hundred and twenty years." (NKJV)

Prayer points:
1. May I leave the number of years that you have ordained for man – one hundred and twenty years in Jesus name.
2. May the years that I live be fruitful in your service in Jesus name. Amen
3. May the years be without sickness in Jesus name
4. May the years not be years of shame in Jesus name
5. May the years that I live glorify your Holy name in Jesus name
6. May I not bring reproach to your name in these years that I shall live in Jesus name

Genesis 6: 5 – Then the Lord saw that the wickedness of man was great in the earth and that every intent of the thoughts of his heart was only evil continually. (NKJV)

Prayer points:
1. Every wickedness in me, I cast you out in Jesus name.
2. Lord Jesus, may every intent of my thoughts not be evil. Amen

3. May every intent of my thoughts be controlled by the Holy Spirit in Jesus name

Genesis 6: 8 & 9, 22 – But Noah found grace in the eyes of the Lord. This is the genealogy of Noah. Noah was a just man, perfect in his generation. Noah walked with God. Thus Noah did; according to all that God commanded him, so he did. (NKJV)

Prayer points:
1. Father, may I find grace in your eyes.
2. Lord Jesus, I want to be perfect in my generation.
3. Father, may I walk with you continually in Jesus name. Amen
4. Lord Jesus grant that I may be a just man/woman
5. Lord Jesus, may I do according to all that God has commanded me
6. Grant Lord that I will obey the 10 commandments in Jesus name. Amen.

Genesis Chapter 7

Genesis 7:1 – Then the Lord said to Noah, "Come into the ark, you and all your household, because I have seen that you are righteous before Me in this generation." (NKJV)

Prayer points:
1. Father, I want to be righteous before you in my generation.
2. I want you to bless me and protect my family and I in Jesus name. Amen.
3. Father hide my family and I under your shadow
4. Father may I find favor with you continually
5. I receive your invitation to 'come' in Jesus name

Genesis Chapter 8

Genesis 8: 20 – Then Noah built an altar to the Lord, and took of every clean animal and of every clean bird, and offered burnt offerings on the altar. And the Lord smelled a soothing aroma. (NKJV)

Prayer points:
1. Wherever I am, may I build an altar to my God in Jesus name.
2. May I continually offer clean sacrifice of praise and worship to my God.
3. May my sacrifice ascend unto you Lord as a sweet aroma
4. God inhabit my praise and worship.
5. Father inhabit my heart
6. Father make a permanent habitation in my home
7. May my desire be to please you in Jesus name
8. May my desire be to do your will in Jesus name
9. May my desire be to dwell in your presence in Jesus name

Genesis Chapter 9

Genesis 9: 2 – And the fear of you and the dread of you shall be on every beast of the earth, on every bird of the air, on all that move on the earth, and on all the fish of the sea. They are given into our hand. (NKJV)

Prayer points:
1. The fear of me shall be on every beast of the earth and on every one of my enemies.
2. The dread of me shall be on my enemies and on every beast and every living thing.
3. I will have dominion over every living thing.
4. No living thing in the physical or in the spiritual will be able to withstand me.

5. No living thing in the physical realm or in the spiritual realm will be able to harm me for God has given me authority and power over them.
6. I stand by the word of God for my life.
7. I claim the promise of God for me.
8. I will be fruitful in accordance to the word of God.
9. I will multiply in accordance to the word of God.
10. I will bring forth abundantly in Jesus name.
11. Whatsoever I shall lay my hands on shall prosper in Jesus name. Amen.

Genesis Chapter 12

Genesis 12: 2-4 & 17 – "I will make you a great nation; I will bless you and make your name great; and you shall be a blessing. I will bless those who bless you. And I will curse him who curse you. And in you all the families of the earth shall be blessed." So Abram departed as the Lord had spoken to him … But the Lord plagued Pharaoh and his house with great plagues because of Sarai, Abram's wife. (NKJV)

Prayer points:
1. Father, make me a great nation
2. Father, bless me
3. Father, make my name great
4. Father, make me a blessing
5. Father, bless those that bless me
6. Father, curse those that curse me
7. Father, may families be blessed by me
8. Father, may I be obedient to your word and your commands in Jesus name. Amen.
9. Father, may I hear you whenever you speak to me.
10. Father, plague my enemies and their households on my behalf for your name sake.

Genesis Chapter 13

Prayer points:
1. May I be rich in silver
2. May I be rich in gold
3. May I prosper in all that I lay my hand on
4. Father enlarge my coast
5. I come against spirit of strife
6. Give me wisdom to deal with strife
7. Give me grace to seek peace
8. May I not be moved by what I see, but by your spirit
9. Open my spiritual eyes that I may see in the spiritual
10. I receive the spirit of discernment

Genesis Chapter 14

Prayer points:
1. May I be able to render help to my brethren when they need help
2. May help not be far from me when I need help
3. Give me wisdom to defend and fight for my brethren
4. May I defeat my enemies and the enemies of my brethren
5. Deliver my enemies into my hand
6. Give me strength and favor to recover all that the enemy has stolen
7. May I praise you oh God for all the victory
8. May I give you oh God all the glory

Genesis Chapter 15

Genesis 15: 1b, 6, & 15b – I am your shield, your exceedingly great reward. 6 – And he believed in the Lord and He accounted it to him for righteousness. 15b – you shall be buried at a good old age. (NKJV)

Prayer points:
1. Father, thank you for your word concerning me, that you are my shield.
2. Thank you Father God for being my exceedingly great reward
3. Father, I desire to believe every word that you speak to me in Jesus name. Amen.
4. Father, I will be buried in good old age in accordance to your word in Jesus name. Amen.

Genesis Chapter 16

Prayer points:
1. I come against the spirit of barreness
2. I will be fruitful
3. I will multiply
4. I will not take the place of God
5. I will let go and let God
6. Spirit of impatience I come against you
7. I receive patience
8. I will wait for God
9. Though the vision may tarry, I will wait
10. May I not be weary in waiting

Genesis Chapter 17

Genesis 17: 1b, & 8 – I am Almighty God; walk before Me and be blameless. 8 – "Also I give to you and your descendants after you the land in which you are a stranger, all the land of Canaan, as an everlasting possession; and I will be their God." (NKJV)

Prayer points:
1. Father, I want to walk before you.
2. Father, I want to be blameless in your sight
3. Father, give unto me and unto my seed after me this land, where I am for an everlasting possession.

4. Father be my God
5. Father be the God of my seed after me.

Genesis Chapter 18

Prayer points:
1. Father may I not miss any opportunity that comes my way
2. Position me in the right place at the right time
3. May I not fail to discern your presence
4. May I understand every sign that you present before me
5. May I not fail to entertain angels that you send my way
6. Father I receive your words for me
7. Forgive every unbelief/doubt in me
8. Father do not hide the things you do from me
9. Father may I command my children and household after you, to serve you oh Lord
10. May I command my household to be just
11. Father bring to pass all that you have promised me

Genesis Chapter 19

Genesis 19: 11 & 16 – And they struck the men who were at the doorway of the house with blindness, both small and great, so that they became weary trying to find the door. 16 – And while he lingered, the men took hold of his hand, his wife's hand, and the hands of his two daughters, the Lord being merciful to him, and they brought him out and set him outside the city. (NKJV)

Prayer points:
1. Father, strike my enemies with blindness
2. My enemies will be weary trying to find me.
3. Father, be merciful to me.
4. Let your angels take hold of my hand, the hand of my daughter and the hand of my son and take us out of the

danger, oppression and bondage that we are in, in Jesus name. Amen.

5. Let your angels take hold of my hand and that of every member of my household and take us out of the danger, oppression and bondage that we are in, in Jesus name

Genesis Chapter 21

Genesis 21: 1 & 6 – And the Lord visited Sarah as He had said and the Lord did for Sarah as He had spoken. 6 – And Sarah said, "God has made me laugh, and all who heard will laugh with me. (NKJV)

Prayer points:
1. God visit me as you said
2. God do to me as you have promised
3. God make me laugh
4. Let all who hear my laughter laugh with me.

Genesis Chapter 24

Genesis 24: 1 – Now Abraham was old, well advanced in age; and the Lord had blessed Abraham in all things. (NKJV)

Prayer points:
1. Father may I live to good old age
2. Father may I be well advanced in age
3. Father bless me in all things. Amen.

Genesis Chapter 26

Genesis 26: 2, 12 – 13 – Then the Lord appeared to him and said, "Do not go down to Egypt; live in the land of which I shall tell you. 12-13 – Then Isaac sowed in that land and reaped in the same year a hundredfold; and the Lord blessed him. The man began to prosper, and continued prospering until he became very prosperous. (NKJV)

Prayer points:
1. Lord appear to me
2. Lord give me instructions
3. Lord may I obey every instruction that you give me.
4. Lord like Isaac sowed in that land and reaped in the same year a hundredfold, may I sow and reap in the same year
5. Like you prospered Isaac, prosper me
6. Like Isaac, may I continue to prosper until I become very prosperous in Jesus name. Amen.

Genesis Chapter 30

Genesis 30:1 & 24 – Now when Rachel saw that she bore Jacob no children, Rachel envied her sister … 24 – The Lord shall add to me another son. (NKJV)

Prayer points:

1. Father, in the name of Jesus I come against every spirit of envy.
2. Spirit of envy, you will not have dominion over me in Jesus name. Amen.
3. Whatever I decree in accordance to the will of God for my life, let it come to pass just as Rachel decreed that God shall add to her another son, so shall it be for me in Jesus name.

Genesis Chapter 31

Genesis 31: 24 – But God had come to Laban the Syrian in a dream by night, and said to him, "Be careful that you speak to Jacob neither good nor bad." (NKJV)

Prayer points:
1. Father, speak to my enemies concerning me that they speak to me neither good nor bad in Jesus name. Amen.

2. Father, warn my enemies and they that plan evil against me that they not trouble me in Jesus name. Amen.

Genesis Chapter 35

Genesis 35: 5 – And they journeyed, and the terror of God was upon the cities that were all around them, and they did not pursue the sons of Jacob. (NKJV)

Prayer point:
1. Father, may your terror be upon my enemies that they trouble me no more in Jesus name. Amen.
2. My enemies, stop pursuing me in Jesus name

Genesis Chapter 38

Genesis 38: 7, 21 & 24b – But Er, Judah's firstborn, was wicked in the sight of the Lord and the Lord killed him. 21 – Then he asked the men of that place saying, "Where is the harlot who was openly by the roadside?" 24 – So Judah said, "Bring her out and let her be burned. (NKJV)

Prayer points:
1. Father, deliver me from every spirit of wickedness in Jesus name.
2. Chastise me not in your anger oh Lord.
3. Father, I come against the spirit of harlotry in our society in Jesus name. Amen.
4. Father, deliver us/me from unjust judges.
5. Father, deliver us/me from the hand of hypocrites in Jesus name. Amen.

Genesis Chapter 39

Genesis 39: 2, 3, 10, 13 & 14 – The Lord was with Joseph, and he was a successful man... 3 – And his master saw that the Lord was with him and that the Lord made all he did to prosper in his hand. 10 – So it was, as she spoke to Joseph day by day, that he did not heed her, to lie with her or to be with her. 13 & 14 – And so it was, when she saw that he had left his garment in her hand and fled outside, that she called to the men of her house and spoke to them saying, "See, he has brought in to us a Hebrew to mock us. He came in to me to lie with me and I cried out with a loud voice. And it happened, when he heard that I lifted my voice and cried out, that he left his garment with me, and fled and went outside." (NKJV)

Prayer points:
1. When the Lord is with you, you will be successful. Lord be with me that I may be successful in Jesus name.
2. Father no matter the pressures of life, may I not sin against you.
3. May I not bring reproach to your holy name in Jesus name.
4. God deliver me from every lie of the enemy in Jesus name.
5. Lord, deliver me from every manipulation of men against me in Jesus name.

Genesis Chapter 39

Genesis 39: 20 -21, 23b – Then Joseph's master took him and put him into prison, a place where the king's prisoners were confined. And he was there in the prison. 21 – But the Lord was with Joseph and showed him favor in the sight of the keeper of the prison. 23b – and whatever he did, the Lord make it prosper. (NKJV)

Prayer points:
1. Father God, be with me that I may be successful in Jesus name. Amen.
2. Father, no matter the pressures of life, may I not sin against you.
3. May I not bring reproach to your holy name in Jesus name.
4. God deliver me from every lie and manipulation of men against me in Jesus name. Amen.
5. Father, be with me in every situation in Jesus name.

6. Give me favor in the camp of my enemies in Jesus name.
7. Father, prosper the works of my hands in Jesus name.
8. Father, deliver me from pride that will hinder my blessings in Jesus name. Amen.

Genesis Chapter 40

Genesis 40:18 – So Joseph answered and said, "This is the interpretation of it: The three baskets are three days. Within three days Pharaoh will lift off your head from you and hang you on a tree; and the birds will eat your flesh from you." (NKJV)

Prayer points:
1. Father, I pray that no matter the circumstance or the situation, may I speak the truth.
2. Father, baptize me with the spirit of truth.
3. Sanctify me, Lord, in your word, for your word is true.

Genesis Chapter 41

Genesis 41: 9-10, 33 – Then the chief butler spoke to Pharaoh, saying: "I remember my faults this day. 10 – When Pharaoh was angry with his servants, and put me in custody in the house of the captain of the guard, both me and the chief baker... 33 – Now therefore, let Pharaoh select a discerning and wise man, and set him over the land of Egypt. Let Pharaoh do this, and let him appoint officers over the land, to collect one-fifth of the produce of the land of Egypt in the seven plentiful years." (NKJV)

Prayer points:

1. Father, let there be a day of remembrance for me.
2. Father, let there be a day you will remember me and deliver me from my enemies in Jesus name. Amen.
3. Father, give me wisdom to manage wealth.

4. Give me wisdom to manage whatever you have placed in my hand – marriage, children, job, money, prayer group etc. in Jesus name.

Genesis Chapter 42

Genesis 42: 1 & 2 – When Jacob saw that there was grain in Egypt; Jacob said to his sons, "Why do you look at one another?" 2 – And he said, "Indeed I have heard that there is grain in Egypt; go down to that place and buy for us there, that we may live and not die."(NKJV)

Prayer points:
1. Father, when you open my eyes to see an opportunity, may I not just sit down and wait for the opportunity to come to me
2. Father, may I have the wisdom, the strength, the capability and the ability to get up and go for the opportunity that you have opened my eyes to see in Jesus name. Amen.

Genesis Chapter 46

Genesis 46: 2 – Then God spoke to Israel in the visions of the night, and said, "Jacob, Jacob!" And he said, "Here I am." (NKJV)

1. Father speak to me in the visions of the night.
2. Father may I continually offer sacrifice to you in the name of Jesus
3. Father may I hear and answer you when you speak to me in Jesus name.

Exodus Chapter 2

Exodus 2: 23 – And it came to pass in process of time, that the king of Egypt died: and the children of Israel sighed by reason of the bondage, and they cried, and their cry came up unto God by reason of the bondage. (NKJV)

Prayer points:
1. Father every enemy that seeks my life and the life of my children will die like pharaoh in Jesus name. Amen.
2. Father, let my cry come up unto you in Jesus name. Amen.
3. Father, save me in Jesus name. Amen.

Exodus Chapter 3

Exodus 3: 4, 7-8 –And when the Lord saw that he turned aside to see, God called unto him out of the midst of the bush, and said, Moses, Moses. And he said, Here am I. 7- And the Lord said, I have surely seen the affliction of my people which are in Egypt, and have heard their cry by reason of their taskmasters; for I know their sorrows; 8 – And I am come down to deliver them out of the hand of the Egyptians, and to bring them up out of that land unto a good land and a large land, unto a land flowing with milk and honey; unto a place of the Canaanites, and the Hittites, and the Amorites, and the Perizzites, and the Hivites, and the Jebusites. (KJV)

Prayer points:
1. Father, may I hear you when you call me in Jesus name. Amen
2. Father, speak to me in Jesus name. Amen.
3. Father, you have seen my afflictions, you have heard my cry, you know my sorrows, come down and deliver me O Lord in Jesus name. Amen.
4. God bring me up from oppression to a good and large land, to a land flowing with milk and honey in Jesus name. Amen.
5. Father, may I not fail to serve you even after you deliver me in Jesus name. Amen.

Exodus Chapter 4

Exodus 4: 19 – Now the Lord said to Moses in Midian, "Go, return to Egypt; for all the men who sought your life are dead." (NKJV)

Prayer points:
1. Father, may all the men who seek my life like pharaoh did Moses, die in Jesus name. Amen

Exodus Chapter 7

Exodus 7: 6-7, 12 & 15 – Then Moses and Aaron did so; just as the Lord commanded them, so they did. 7- And Moses was eighty years old and Aaron eighty-three years old when they spoke to Pharaoh. 12- For every man threw down his rod, and they became serpents. But Aaron's rod swallowed up their rods. 15 – "Go to Pharaoh in the morning when he goes out to the water. (NKJV)

Prayer points:
1. Father, may I do just as you command me in Jesus name. Amen
2. Father, may I live to a good old age in Jesus name. Amen
3. May I serve you actively in my good old age in Jesus name. Amen
4. May I hear you clearly, when you speak in Jesus name.
5. May I see you clearly
6. May the power of God in me defeat and overthrow every evil power troubling me in Jesus name.
7. Strengthen me Lord to seek you early in the morning, even before my enemies prophesy into my day. Amen

Exodus Chapter 14

Exodus 14: 13 & 14 – And Moses said unto the people, fear ye not, stand still, and see the salvation of the Lord, which he will shew to you to day; for the Egyptians whom ye have seen to day, ye shall see them again no more for ever. 14 – The Lord shall fight for you, and ye shall hold your peace. (KJV)

Prayer points:
1. I will not fear in Jesus name. Amen
2. I will stand still for God to fight for me in Jesus name
3. I will see the salvation of the Lord in Jesus name
4. Every oppressor, every trouble that represents the Egyptians in my life that I see today, I will not see again forever in Jesus name.
5. The Lord will fight for me and I will hold my peace in Jesus name. Amen.

Exodus Chapter 15

Exodus 15: 26 – And said, if thou wilt diligently hearken to the voice of the Lord thy God, and wilt do that which is right in his sight, and wilt give ear to his commandments, and keep all his statues, I will put none of these diseases upon thee, which I have brought upon the Egyptians: for I am the Lord that healeth thee. (KJV)

Prayer points:
1. I will hearken to the voice of the Lord my God in Jesus name.
2. I will do that which is right in the sight of My God in Jesus name
3. I will give ear to the commandments of my God in Jesus name
4. I will keep all the statutes of my God in Jesus name
5. I will not have the diseases of the Egyptians in the name of Jesus
6. Lord heal me of every sickness and disease in Jesus name.

Leviticus Chapter 6

Leviticus 6: 12 – 13. And the fire upon the alter shall be burning in it; it shall not be put out: and the priest shall burn wood on it every morning, and lay the burnt offering in order upon it; and he shall burn thereon the fat of the peace offerings. 13 – The fire shall ever be burning upon the altar; it shall never go out. (KJV)

Prayer points:
1. Father let the fire of prayer burn continuously in me in Jesus name
2. Let me receive fresh baptism of prayer every morning in Jesus name
3. May I enter your gate with thanksgiving in my heart.
4. May I enter your court with praise.
5. This is the day that the Lord has made.
6. I will rejoice in this day and be glad in Jesus name
7. May the fire of prayer in my life burn continuously and never go out in Jesus name.

Numbers Chapter 1

Prayer points:

1. Father, I pray that like Moses, I will obey your commandment to the latter. Speak to me Lord, in Jesus name. Amen.

Numbers Chapter 3

Numbers 3: 4- And Nadab and Abihu died before the Lord, when they offered strange fire before the Lord, in the wilderness of Sinai, and they had no children. (KJV)

Prayer points:
1. Father, may I not offer strange fire before you in Jesus name.
2. May I not die childless in Jesus name.
3. May I be obedient to your word in Jesus name.
4. Anoint my ears to hear you when you speak in Jesus name
5. Anoint my mouth to speak your words in Jesus name.
6. Anoint my eyes to see beyond the physical in Jesus name.
7. Father, like Moses, may I obey your commandment to the latter in Jesus name. Amen.

Deuteronomy Chapter 32

Deuteronomy 32:12 &13 – So the Lord alone did lead him, and there was no strange god with him. He made him ride on high places of the earth, that he might eat the increase of the fields; and he made him to suck honey out of the rock, and oil out of the flinty rock. (KJV)

Prayer points:
1. Father, lead me in Jesus name
2. Make me ride on the high places of the earth in Jesus name
3. May I eat the increase of the fields in Jesus name
4. God do the impossible in my life
5. God do the impossible in my marriage
6. God do the impossible in my health
7. God do the impossible in everything that concerns me
8. God do the impossible in my spiritual life
9. God do the impossible in my church
10. God do the impossible in my home
11. God bring honey out of the rock for me to suck
12. God fill me with the Holy Spirit and with power in Jesus name. Amen.

Deuteronomy Chapter 33

Deuteronomy 33: 27 – The eternal God is thy refuge, and underneath are the everlasting arms: and he shall thrust out the enemy from before thee; and shall say, Destroy them. (KJV)

Prayer points:
1. Father God, you are my refuge
2. Father underneath are your everlasting arms
3. Father thrust out the enemy from before me.
4. Father destroy my enemies in Jesus name. Amen

Joshua Chapter 1

Joshua 1: 3, 5 – 6, 7 - 9 - Every place that the sole of your foot shall tread upon, that have I given unto you, as I said unto Moses. 5 – There shall not any man be able to stand before thee all the days of thy life: as I was with Moses, so I will be with thee: I will not fail thee, nor forsake thee. 6 – Be strong and of good courage: ... 7 – Only be thou strong and very courageous, that thou mayest observe to do according to all the law, which Moses my servant commanded thee: turn not from it to the right hand or to the left, that thou mayest prosper whithersoever thou goest. 8 – This book of the law shall not depart out of thy mouth; but thou shalt meditate therein day and night, that thou mayest obseve to do according to all that is written therein: for then thou shalt make thy way prosperous, and then thou shalt have good success. 9 – Have not I commanded thee? Be strong and of a good courage, be not afraid, neither be thou dismayed: for the Lord thy God is with thee whithersoever thou goest. (KJV)

Prayer points:

1. Father give me every place that the sole of my feet have treaded upon in accordance to your word in Jesus name.
2. Father may no one be able to stand before me all the days of my life in Jesus name
3. Father, be with me as you were with Moses in Jesus name
4. Father, do not fail me because you fail no man in Jesus name
5. Father, forsake me not because you forsake no man in Jesus name
6. I pray for the grace to be strong in Jesus name
7. I pray for the grace to be of good courage in Jesus name
8. Help me, Holy Spirit, to observe to do according to all the commandments of the Lord in Jesus name.
9. May I not turn from your commandment to the right hand or to the left hand in Jesus name.

10. May I prosper in all that I do in Jesus name.
11. May I prosper wherever I go in Jesus name
12. May your word not depart from my mouth in Jesus name
13. May I meditate upon your word day and night
14. May I do according to all that is written in your word in Jesus name
15. May my ways be prosperous
16. May I have good success
17. Spirit of fear I come against you in Jesus name
18. May I not be dismayed in Jesus name
19. I receive strength in Jesus name
20. I receive spirit of courage in Jesus name.
21. Spirit of fear and dismay, I cast you out of my life in Jesus name.
22. I receive what I confess that I will receive in the name of Jesus.
23. I receive abundant strength in Jesus name.
24. I receive outstanding divine favor in Jesus name.
25. I receive permanent healing in Jesus name
26. Every organ in my body that is not functioning well, I command you in the name of Jesus to begin to function in Jesus name.
27. Every weak organ in my body, receive strength in Jesus name.
28. Father God, be with me whithersoever I go in Jesus name.
29. Be with me Lord God in the camp of the enemies in Jesus name
30. Father be with me in the camp of friends in Jesus name

Joshua Chapter 4

Joshua 4: 14 – On that day the Lord magnified Joshua in the sight of all Israel; and they feared him, as they feared Moses, all the days of his life. (KJV)

Prayer points:
1. Lord magnify me before my brethren and before men in Jesus name.
2. I will keep the commandment of the Lord continuously in Jesus name.
3. Father, like you dried up the Red sea and river Jordan, dry up every stream, sea and river of hindrance in my way in Jesus name.

Joshua Chapter 5

Joshua 5:1b, 2, & 9 - …that their heart melted, neither was there spirit in them any more, because of the children of Israel. 2 – At that time the Lord said unto Joshua, Make thee sharp knives, and circumcise again the children of Israel the second time. 9 – And the Lord said unto Joshua, This day have I rolled away the reproach of Egypt from off you. (KJV)

Prayer points:
1. The heart of my enemies shall melt when they hear of God's goodness in my life in Jesus name
2. Lord, I rededicate my life to you in Jesus name
3. Father, today, roll away the reproach of my enemies from me in Jesus name. Amen.

Joshua Chapter 10

Joshua 10: 8, 10-13 – And the Lord said unto Joshua, Fear them not: for I have delivered them into thine hand; there shall not a man of them stand before thee. 10 –And the Lord discomfited them before Israel, and slew them with a great slaughter at Gibeon, and chased them along the way that goeth up to Beth-horon, and smote them to Azekah, and unto Makkedah. 11 – And it came to pass, as they fled from before Israel, and were in the going down to Beth-horon, that the Lord cast down great stones from heaven upon them unto

Azekah, and they died: they were more which died with hailstones than they whom the children of Israel slew with the sword. 12 – Then spake, Joshua to the Lord in the day when the Lord delivered up the Amorites before the children of Israel, and he said in the sight of Israel, Sun, stand thou still upon Gibeon; and thou, Moon, in the valley of Ajalon. 13 – And the sun stood still, and the moon stayed, until the people had avenged themselves upon their enemies. (KJV)

Prayer points:
1. Father in accordance to your word, I will not fear in Jesus name.
2. Father, you will deliver my enemies into my hand in Jesus name.
3. None of my enemies will be able to stand before me in Jesus name
4. Lord discomfit my enemies from before me in Jesus name
5. Slay my enemies with a great slaughter in Jesus name
6. Chase my enemies from before me in Jesus name
7. Smite my enemies in Jesus name
8. Lord, cast down great hailstones upon my enemies that they may die in Jesus name
9. Father, give me the boldness to command the works of your hand, to command the sun and the moon to fight on my behalf against my enemies in Jesus name.

Joshua Chapter 11

Joshua 11: 15b - …he left nothing undone of all that the Lord commanded Moses. (KJV)

Prayer points:
1. Father, may I obey your commandment to the latter in Jesus name
2. Father, like Moses, may I not leave anything undone that needs to be done in Jesus name. Amen.

Joshua Chapter 23

Joshua 23: 1, 3, 5 & 10 – And it came to pass a long time after that the Lord had given rest unto Israel from all their enemies round about, that Joshua waxed old and stricken in age. 3b - ...for the Lord your God is he that hath fought for you. 5 – And the Lord your God, he shall expel them from before you, and drive them from out of your sight; and ye shall possess their land, as the Lord your God hath promised unto you. 10 – One man of you shall chase a thousand: for the Lord your God, he it is that fighteth for you, as he hath promised you. (KJV)

Prayer points:
1. Father, let it come to pass in my life that you will give my enemies into my hand and you will give me rest from all my enemies round about me in Jesus name
2. Father, in accordance to your word, may I grow to good old age and wax old and stricken in age in Jesus name.
3. Father, in the name of Jesus, continue to fight for me.
4. Lord Jesus, expel my enemies from before me.
5. Lord Jesus drive my enemies away out of my sight in Jesus name
6. In accordance to your word, Lord, I will possess the lands of my enemies in Jesus name.
7. In accordance to your word Lord, I will chase a thousand in Jesus name.
8. Father, you are the God that fights for me, and you will fight for me and chase my enemies from before my sight in Jesus name.

Judges Chapter 15

Judges 15: 14 – And when he came unto Lehi, the Philistines shouted against him: and the spirit of the Lord came mightily upon him, and the cords that were upon his arms became as flax that was burning with fire, and his hands loosed from off his hands. (KJV)

Prayer points:
1. Father I pray that your spirit will come upon me mightily in Jesus name.
2. Lord I pray that the evil cords that the enemies have used to bind me and my family will loose in the name of Jesus amen
3. Lord I pray that the evil cords of my enemies will become as flax that was burning with fire in Jesus name.
4. Father, loose me and my family from the bondage of the enemies in Jesus name
5. Father, loose the children of God from the bondage of their enemies in Jesus name.
6. Father, disappoint my enemies in Jesus name
7. Anytime my enemies think that they have defeated me, Lord, disappoint my enemies and the enemies of your children in Jesus name. Amen.

Ruth Chapter 2

Ruth 2: 12 & 13 – The Lord recompense thy work, and a full reward be given thee of the Lord God of Israel, under whose wings thou art come to trust. 13 – Then she said, Let me find favor in thy sight, my Lord, for that thou hast comforted me, and for that thou hast spoken friendly unto thine handmaid, though I be not like unto one of thy handmaidens. (KJV)

Prayer points:
1. Lord Jesus, may I be faithful and hardworking in Jesus name.
2. Every spirit of laziness I come against you in Jesus name
3. Every spirit of procrastination I come against you in Jesus name
4. Every spirit of imperfection I come against you in Jesus name

5. Every spirit of ignorance I come against you in Jesus name.
6. Every spirit of slumber I come against you in Jesus name
7. Every spirit of folding of the hands I come against you in Jesus name.
8. Every spirit behind lack of commitment I come against you in Jesus name
9. Every spirit behind shyness when I should be bold I come against you in Jesus name
10. Father, may your favor be upon me in all that I do in Jesus name
11. Father, may your favor go before me wherever and whenever I need it in Jesus name
12. May your favor go with me wherever and whenever I need it in Jesus name
13. May your favor go after me wherever and whenever I need it in Jesus name.

1 Samuel Chapter 2

1 Samuel 2: 2, 6 – 10, 26 – There is none holy as the Lord: for there is none beside thee: neither is there any rock like our God. 6 – The Lord killeth, and maketh alive: he bringeth down to the grave, and bringeth up. 7 – The Lord maketh poor, and maketh rich: he bringeth low and lifteth up. 8 – He raiseth up the poor out of the dust, and lifteth up the beggar from the dunghill, to set them among princes, and to make them inherit the throne of glory: for the pillars of the earth are the Lord's, and he hath set the world upon them. 9 – He will keep the feet of his saints, and the wicked shall be silent in darkness, for by strength shall no man prevail. 10 – The adversaries of the Lord shall be broken to pieces, out of heaven shall he thunder upon them: the Lord shall give strength unto his king, and exalt the horn of his anointed. 26 – And the child Samuel grew on, and was in favor both with the Lord and also with men. (KJV)

Prayer points:

1. Father, there is none holy as you Lord
2. Father, there is none besides you.
3. Father there is no rock like you
4. You are the great and mighty God
5. You are the God that killeth
6. You are the God that maketh alive
7. You are the God that bringeth to the grave
8. You are the God that bringeth up.
9. There is none like you Lord
10. You are the Lord that can make poor
11. Your are the Lord that can make rich
12. You are the Lord that bringeth low
13. It is only you Lord that can raise the poor out of the dust
14. Father raise me out of the dust in Jesus name
15. God alone can raise the beggar out of the dunghill.
16. Lord in Jesus name, raise me out of the dunghill.
17. Lord set me among princes and princesses because you alone can make it happen
18. Lord make me to inherit the throne of glory in Jesus name.
19. Nothing is too difficult for you
20. Nothing is impossible for you except to lie
21. Father, in accordance to your word, keep my feet in Jesus name.
22. Father God, silence the wicked in Jesus name.
23. Lord, silence my enemies in Jesus name.
24. Lord, may your adversaries be broken into pieces
25. Father, your adversaries are my adversaries and my adversaries are your adversaries, therefore, may our adversaries be broken in pieces in Jesus name.
26. May it thunder out of heaven upon our adversaries in Jesus name. Amen
27. Father, you are the impartial judge, judge the ends of the earth in accordance to your word in Jesus name
28. Father God, give strength unto me in Jesus name.

29. Father, give strength unto your children in Jesus name
30. Father, give strength unto the people of God in Jesus name. Amen.
31. Father, may I grow in you Lord in Jesus name.
32. Father, may I find favor in you in Jesus name.
33. Father, may I find favor with men in Jesus name. Amen.
34. Father, may I honor you in Jesus name.
35. Father, may I honor you in my thoughts
36. Father, may I honor you with my words
37. Father, may I honor you in my deeds
38. Father, may I honor you in all that I do in Jesus name
39. Father, may I not despise you in Jesus name. Amen.

1 Samuel Chapter 3

1 Samuel 3: 11 – And the Lord said to Samuel, Behold, I will do a thing in Israel, at which both the ears or every one that heareth it shall tingle. (KJV)

Prayer points:
1. Father, do a new thing in my life that every ear that heareth shall tingle in Jesus name.
2. Father, do a new thing in my health that every ear that hears will tingle in Jesus name.
3. Father, do a new thing in my spiritual life that every ear that hears will tingle in Jesus name.
4. Father, do a new thing in my family that every ear that hears will tingle in Jesus name.
5. Father, do a new thing at my job for me so that every ear that hears will tingle in Jesus name.

1 Samuel Chapter 7

1 Samuel 7: 10 – And as Samuel was offering up the burnt offering, the Philistines drew near to battle against Israel: but the Lord thundered

with a great thunder on that day upon the Philistines, and discomfited them; and they were smitten before Israel. (KJV)

Prayer points:
1. Father, may I offer sacrifice of praise to you.
2. Father, may I offer sacrifice of thanksgiving to you.
3. Father, may I offer sacrifice of adoration to you in Jesus name.
4. Father, as many times as the enemy is drawing near to battle against me, Lord, let your thunder come upon them greatly in Jesus name
5. Father, discomfit my enemies that are drawing near to battle against me in Jesus name.
6. Father, smite my enemies that are drawing near to battle against me in Jesus name. Amen.

1 Samuel Chapter 17

1 Samuel 17: 37, 45 - 47 – David said moreover, The Lord that delivered me out of the paw of the lion, and out of the paw of the bear, he will deliver me out of the hand of this Philistine. 45 – Then said David to the Philistine, Thou comest to me with a sword, and with spear, and with a shield: but I come to thee in the name of the Lord of hosts, the God of the armies of Israel, whom thou hast defiled. 46 – This day will the Lord deliver thee into mine hand; and I will smite thee, and take thine head from thee; and I will give the carcasses of the host of the Philistines this day unto the fowls of the air, and to the wild beasts of the earth; that all the earth may know that there is a God in Israel. 47 – And all this assembly shall know that the Lord saveth not with sword, and spear: for the battle is the Lord's, and he will give you into our hands. (KJV)

Prayer points:
1. Thank you Father in heaven for your past deliverance from the hands of my enemies in Jesus name

2. God I know and believe that you are the same yesterday, today and forever.
3. Father, deliver me from the hands of my enemies that trouble my soul in Jesus name.
4. Hear this devil, God Almighty, The MAN of war He is the power behind me in Jesus name.
5. Father, deliver my enemies into my hands this day in Jesus name.
6. Father, smite my enemies that all the earth will know that I serve a living God
7. Father God all will know that you are able to deliver your children.
8. Father all will know that the battle is the Lord's

1 Samuel Chapter 18

1 Samuel 18: 12 – And Saul was afraid of David, because the Lord was with him, and was departed from Saul. (KJV).

Prayer points:
1. Father, may the enemies be afraid of me in Jesus name. Amen
2. May my enemies see clearly that God Almighty is with me and be afraid of me in Jesus name.

1 Samuel Chapter 19

1 Samuel 19: 10 – And Saul sought to smite David even to the wall with the javelin; but he slipt away out of Saul's presence, and he smote the javelin into the wall; and David fled, and escaped that night. (KJV)

Prayer points:
1. God will protect me continuously from my enemies in Jesus name

2. Any time the enemy tries to kill me, I will slip away from my enemy in Jesus name
3. Anytime my enemies try to harm me, I will slip away from them in Jesus name.
4. Anytime my enemies try to harm me, they will hit the wall in Jesus name
5. God will cause me to escape from the sword of the enemies in Jesus name.
6. God will cause me to escape from every danger and harm in my way in Jesus name.

1 Samuel Chapter 25

1 Samuel 25: 24, 29, 39b – And fell at his feet, and said, Upon me, my Lord, upon me let this iniquity be: and let thine handmaid, I pray thee, speak in thine audience and hear the words of thine handmaid. 29 – Yet a man is risen to pursue thee, and to see thy soul: but the soul of my lord shall be bound in the bundle of life with the Lord thy God; and the souls of thine enemies, them shall he sling out as out of the middle of a sling. 39b – for the Lord hath returned the wickedness of Nabal upon his own head. (KJV)

Prayer points:
1. In the above scripture, we see that Abigail was interceding on behalf of her husband by saying, "Upon me, my Lord, upon me let this iniquity be". In the same vein, let us learn to intercede on behalf of our family members and friends.
2. Identify with the sins of others and intercede on their behalf in Jesus name.
3. Any man that riseth against me to pursue me, and to seek my soul, will not catch me in Jesus name.
4. My soul shall be bound in the bundle of life with the Lord my God in Jesus name.
5. The soul of my enemies, them shall my God sling out as out of the middle of a sling in Jesus name.

6. My enemies shall be like Nabal whom the Lord will return their wickedness upon their own heads in Jesus name. Amen.

1 Samuel Chapter 26

1 Samuel 26:12 & 21 - So David took the spear and the cruse of water from Saul's bolster; and they gat them away, and no man saw it, nor knew it, neither awaked: for they were all asleep; because a deep sleep from the Lord was fallen upon them. 21 – Then said Saul, I have sinned: return, my son David: for I will no more do thee harm, because my soul was precious in thine eyes this day: behold, I have played the fool, and have erred exceedingly. (KJV)

Prayer points:
1. Father, send a deep sleep upon my enemies that they may be harmless to me and my family in Jesus name.
2. Father, may my enemies that seek after my life accept their folly and repent in Jesus name. Amen.

2 Samuel Chapter 3

2 Samuel 3: 39 – And I am this day weak, though anointed king; and these men the sons of Zeruiah be too hard for me: the Lord shall reward the doer of evil according to his wickedness. (KJV)

Prayer points:
1. Father, any man, any woman, any boy or girl that plans evil against your children; reward them according to their evil in Jesus name.
2. Anyone that will not respect the place of authority that you have placed your children in, reward them according to their evil in Jesus name.
3. Father, any in-law that will not respect the position that you have placed your children, reward them accordingly in Jesus name.

4. Father any in-law that will hinder the clinging of husband and wife in order for them to be one flesh, reward them accordingly.
5. As many as want to bring shame upon your children, Father, let the shame be upon the enemies of your children in Jesus name.
6. Father, your word says that they that put their trust in you shall not be put to shame. May your children not be put to shame in Jesus name.

2 Samuel Chapter 11

2 Samuel 11:1, 8, 11 & 17 – And it came to pass, after the year was expired, at the time when kings go forth to battle, that David sent Joab, and his servants with him, and all Israel; and they destroyed the children of Ammon, and besieged Rabbah. But David tarried still at Jerusalem. 8 – And David said to Uriah, Go down to thy house, and wash thy feet… 11 – And Uriah said unto David, The ark, and Israel, and Judah, abide in tents; and my lord Joab, and the servants of my lord, are encamped in the open fields; shall I then go into mine house, to eat and to drink, and to lie with my wife? As thou livest, and as thy soul liveth, I will not do this thing. 17 – And the men of the city went out, and fought with Joab: and there fell some of the people of the servants of David; and Uriah the Hittite died. (KJV)

Prayer points:
1. Father God, may I take care of my responsibilities in Jesus name.
2. Father, may I not delegate my God-given responsibility to others in Jesus name.
3. May I not sit down idle instead of working for you so that the enemy will not use me as the enemy used David in Jesus name.
4. Father, when I sin, may I repent before you in Jesus name.

5. Father, may I not try to cover or hide my sin because I know that every sin will come into the open.
6. I will not die because of another person's sin in Jesus name
7. Jesus has already died for our sins
8. I will not die in place of another person
9. I will not die because of the wickedness of any man
10. I will not die for any person to cover their sins in Jesus name. Amen.

2 Samuel Chapter 21

2 Samuel 21: 17 – But Abishai the son of Zeruiah succored him, and smote the Philistine, and killed him. Then the men of David swore unto him saying, Thou shalt go no more out with us to battle, that thou quench not the light of Israel. (KJV)

Prayer points:
1. Father, may I not hang out too often with the person that can quench the fire of God in me in Jesus name.
2. Father, lead me to hang out with those that will sharpen me and those that I can sharpen in Jesus name

1 Kings Chapter 5

1 Kings 5:7 – And it came to pass, when Hiram heard the words of Solomon, that he rejoiced greatly, and said, Blessed be the Lord this day, which hath given unto David a wise son over this great people. (KJV)

Prayer points:
1. Father, may the report concerning my children bring me great joy in Jesus name.
2. May my children love and desire to be in your presence in Jesus name.
3. May my children be wise in Jesus name.

1 Kings Chapter 8: 57-61

Prayer points:
1. Father, God be with your children in Jesus name.
2. Father, do not leave us or forsake us in Jesus name.
3. Father, incline our hearts unto you in Jesus name
4. Father, may we walk in all your ways in Jesus name
5. Father, may we obey your commandments in Jesus name.
6. Let our cry and our supplication be before you day and night in Jesus name.
7. Father, favor your children in Jesus name.
8. Father, all the people of the earth shall know that you are our God in Jesus name
9. All the people of the earth shall know that you are God and there is no one else like you in Jesus name
10. Father, may our hearts be perfect in you in Jesus name.

1 Kings Chapter 22

1 Kings 22: 5 & 14 – And Jehoshaphat said unto the king of Israel, Inquire, I pray thee, at the word of the Lord to day. 14 – And Micaiah said, As the Lord liveth, what the Lord saith unto me, that will I speak. (KJV)

Prayer points:
1. Father, may I seek your face before taking any step in life in Jesus name.
2. Father, may I see your face in everything I do in Jesus name.
3. May I obey your command after seeking your face.
4. Father, may I speak only the words you ask me to speak in Jesus name.

2 Kings Chapter 1

2 Kings 1: 4, 6b, & 10 – Now therefore thus saith the Lord, Thou shalt not come down from that bed on which thou art gone up, but shalt surely die. And Elijah departed. 6b - ...therefore thou shalt not come down from that bed on which thou art gone up, but shalt surely die. 10 – And Elijah answered and said to the captain in fifty, If I be a man of God, then let fire come down from heaven, and consume thee and thy fifty. And there came down fire from heaven, and consumed him and his fifty. (KJV)

Prayer points:
1. My enemies shall go up upon the bed of sickness and shall not come down in Jesus name.
2. Father, may the words that come out of my mouth come with power and with anointing in Jesus name. Amen.

2 Kings Chapter 3

2 Kings 3:22 & 23 – And they rose up early in the morning, and the sun shone upon the water, and the Moabites saw the water on the other side as red as blood: 23 – And they said, This is blood: the kings are surely slain, and they have smitten one another: now therefore, Moab, to the spoil. (KJV)

Prayer points:
1. Father, send confusion into the camp of my enemies in Jesus name.
2. When my enemies see water, let them think it is blood in Jesus name.
3. When they hear laughter, let them think it is crying.
4. When they hear rejoicing let them think it is mourning in Jesus name.

2 Kings Chapter 13

2 Kings 13: 4 – And Jehoshaphat besought the Lord, and the Lord hearkened unto him: for he saw the oppression of Israel, because the king of Syria oppressed them. (KJV)

Prayer points:
1. Father God, I seek your face this morning.
2. Father harken unto me Lord God
3. Father, see the oppression of my enemies upon me
4. Father, deliver me and my family from oppression in Jesus name. Amen

2 Kings Chapter 17

2 Kings 17: 20 & 24 – And the Lord rejected all the seed of Israel, and afflicted them, and delivered them into the hand of spoilers, until he had cast them out of his sight. 24 – And the king of Assyria brought men from Babylon, and from Cuthah, and from Ava, and from Hamath, and from Sepharvaim, and placed them in the cities of Samaria instead of the children of Israel: and they possessed Samaria, and dwelt in the cities thereof. (KJV)

Prayer points:
1. Father, may my enemies not possess my possession.
2. May I walk in your ways continually in Jesus name
3. May I obey your commandments in Jesus name
4. Father, deliver my enemies into the hand of spoilers.
5. Father, cast my enemies out from before me in Jesus name.

2 Kings Chapter 19

2 Kings 19: 6, 15 – 19 & 35 – And Isaiah said unto them, Thus shall ye say to your master, Thus saith the Lord, Be not afraid of the words which thou hast heard, with which the servants of the king of Assyria have blasphemed me... 35 – And it came to pass that night, that the

angel of the Lord went out, and smote in the camp of the Assyrians an hundred fourscore and five thousand: and when they arose early in the morning, behold, they were all dead corpses. (KJV)

Prayer points:
1. I will not be afraid of the words of my enemies in Jesus name
2. Father, send a blast upon my enemies.
3. Let my enemies hear a rumor and turn back from pursuing me.
4. Let my enemies hear a rumor and turn back from afflicting me.
5. God cause my enemies to fall by their own sword. Amen.
6. Father, defend me and my family against my enemies for your name sake in Jesus name.
7. Father, send your angels out by night to smite my enemies in their numbers.
8. Let my enemies all become dead corpses in Jesus name.

2 Kings Chapter 20

2 Kings 20: 5 – ..., Thus saith the Lord, the God of David thy father, I have heard thy prayer, I have seen thy tears: behold, I will heal thee: on the third day thou shalt go up unto the house of the Lord. (KJV)

Prayer points:
1. Father, hear my prayers in Jesus name.
2. Father, see my tears in Jesus name.
3. Father, heal me in Jesus name. Amen.

2 Chronicles Chapter 1

2 Chronicles 1:1 – And Solomon the son of David was strengthened in his kingdom, and the Lord his God was with him, and magnified him exceedingly. (KJV)

Prayer points:
1. Father God, give me wisdom.
2. Father God, magnify me exceedingly in Jesus name

3. Father God, appear unto me and ask me what you shall give me like Solomon in Jesus name.
4. Give me wisdom, Lord, knowledge, understanding and the fear of God in Jesus name. Amen.

2 Chronicles Chapter 5

2 Chronicles 5: 14 – So that the priests could not stand to minister by reason of the cloud: for the glory of the Lord had filled the house of God. (KJV)

Prayer points:
1. Father, be the minister in our midst.
2. Father, let your glory fill us your temple in Jesus name. Amen.

2 Chronicles Chapter 19

2 Chronicles 19: 1 – And Jehoshaphat the King of Judah returned to his house in peace to Jerusalem. (KJV)

Prayer points:
1. Father, whenever I go out, may I return to my house in peace in Jesus name.
2. Peace shall make a permanent habitation in my home in Jesus name.
3. Peace shall be a citizen of my home in Jesus name. Amen.

2 Chronicles Chapter 20

2 Chronicles 20: 3-4, 15b, 17, 20b, 21b & 27 – And Jehoshaphat feared, and set himself to seek the Lord, and proclaimed a fast throughout all Judah. 4 – And Judah gathered themselves together, to ask help of the Lord: even out of all the cities of Judah they came to seek the Lord. 15b – Thus saith the Lord unto you, Be not afraid nor dismayed by reason of this great multitude; for the battle is not yours, but God's. 17 – Ye shall not need to fight in this battle: set yourselves, stand

ye still, and see the salvation of the Lord with you, O Judah and Jerusalem: fear not, nor be dismayed; to morrow go out against them: for the Lord will be with you. 20b – Believe in the Lord your God, so shall you be established; believe his prophets, so shall ye prosper. 21b – Praise the Lord; for his mercy endureth for ever. 27 – Then they returned, every man of Judah and Jerusalem, and Jehoshaphat in the forefront of them, to go again to Jerusalem with joy; for the Lord had made them to rejoice over their enemies. (KJV)

Prayer points:
1. Father, like Jehoshaphat, let fear drive me to set myself to seek you in the name of Jesus.
2. Father when seeking your face, may I also fast in Jesus name.
3. Father, may I ask you for help and not ask man in Jesus name.
4. Father, in accordance to your word to your children when faced with their enemies, I will not fear in Jesus name.
5. I will not be afraid in Jesus name
6. I will not be dismayed because of my enemies in Jesus name.
7. Father the battle that I am involved in is not mine Lord, but God's.
8. Father, I will not need to fight this battle in accordance to your word in Jesus name.
9. Father, I will stand still in Jesus name.
10. I will see the salvation of the Lord with me in Jesus name
11. I will not be afraid nor dismayed in Jesus name
12. Father God, you will be with me in Jesus name.
13. Father, I believe in you my Lord God.
14. I will be established because I believe in the Lord my God
15. I will believe the prophets of the Lord and I will prosper in accordance to the word of God.
16. Lord, I praise you in Jesus name
17. Lord, your mercy endureth forever.
18. Father, make me rejoice over my enemies in Jesus name.
19. Father, set an ambushment against my enemies in Jesus name.

20. My enemies that have come against me, Lord smite them in Jesus name

21. Father, let my enemies fight against one another in Jesus name.

22. Father, let my enemies destroy themselves in Jesus name.

2 Chronicles Chapter 26

2 Chronicles 26: 5 – And he sought God in the days of Zechariah, who had understanding in the visions of God: and as long as he sought the Lord, God made him to prosper. (KJV)

Prayer points:
1. Father, may I seek your face all the days of my life in Jesus name.
2. Father, make me prosper as long as I seek you in Jesus name.

2 Chronicles Chapter 32

2 Chronicles 32: 7-8, 20, 21 – Be strong and courageous, be not afraid nor dismayed for the king of Assyria, nor for all the multitude that is with him: for there be more with us than with him. 8 – With him is an arm of flesh; but with us is the Lord our God to help us, and to fight our battles. 20 – And for this cause Hezekiah the king, and the prophet Isaiah the son of Amoz, prayed and cried to heaven. 21 – And the Lord sent an angel, which cut off all the mighty men of valour, and the leaders and captains in the camp of the king of Assyria. So he retuned with shame of face to his own land. And when he was come into the house of his god, they that came forth of his own bowels slew him there with the sword. (KJV)

Prayer points:
1. Father I will be strong and courageous in Jesus name
2. Father I will not be afraid nor dismayed in Jesus name
3. I will not be afraid of the many enemies that surround me.

4. Father I believe your word that greater is he that is in me than he that is in the world
5. Greater is the power of God in me than the power of the evil one that is in my enemies.
6. Father God, I will not trust in the arm of flesh.
7. I will trust in the Lord my God who is my help in Jesus name.
8. I will trust in the Lord my God who will fight my battle in Jesus name.

Ezra Chapter 3

Ezra 3:1-13

Prayer Points:
1. Father, may we seek your face when fears comes upon us in Jesus name.
2. Father, may we seek your face in the morning and in the evening in Jesus name
3. Lord, we will sing together to you in Jesus name.
4. Lord, we will praise your holy name in Jesus name.
5. Lord, we will give thanks in Jesus name
6. Lord, we will praise and thank you for your goodness in Jesus name.
7. Lord, we praise and thank you for your mercy that endures for ever towards us.

Ezra Chapter 4

Ezra 4: 1-24

Prayer Points:
1. Father, reveal unto us enemies that come in our midst to destroy the work of God in our lives in Jesus name.
2. Expose pretenders in the midst of your people in Jesus name

3. Give us discerning spirit that we will see pretenders in Jesus name
4. May we not allow falsehood in our midst in Jesus name
5. May we not accept help from evil men in Jesus name
6. Give us boldness to say NO to evil help or assistance in Jesus name

Nehemiah Chapter 9

Nehemiah 9: 5b – SONG – Stand up stand up and bless the Lord your God from everlasting, to everlasting. Stand up stand up and bless the Lord your God from everlasting to everlasting. Blessed be your glorious name o Lord, which is exalted above all blessings and praise, blessed be your glorious name o Lord, which is exalted, which is exalted.

Nehemiah Chapter 13

Nehemiah 13: 2 – Because they met not the children of Israel with bread and with water, but hired Balaam against them, that he should curse them: howbeit our God turned the curse into blessing. (KJV)

Prayer points:
1. God, turn the cursing of my enemies to blessing in Jesus name.
2. Father, let every evil planned against me by my enemy turn to good in Jesus name.
3. Every pit that my enemy has dug for me, let it turn to steps that will lead me to my promised land in Jesus name.

Esther Chapter 4

Esther 4: 16 – Go, gather together all the Jews that are present in Shushan, and fast ye for me, and neither eat nor drink three days, night or day; I also and my maidens will fast likewise; and so will I go in unto the king, which is not according to the law: and if I perish, I perish. (KJV)

Prayer points:
1. Father, in the name of Jesus, I pray for the enablement to fast in times of need.
2. Father, I pray for boldness, and the spirit to be selfless, not concerned about my life on earth but the after life in heaven.
3. Father, I pray for the boldness to say like Esther, 'if I perish, I perish".

Esther Chapter 5

Esther 5: 3 – Then said the king unto her, what wilt thou queen Esther? And what is thy request? It shall be even given thee to the half of the kingdom. (KJV)

Prayer points:
1. Father, open doors of opportunity for me in Jesus name.
2. Father, may I find favor with they that are too strong for me.
3. May they that are too strong for me ask me what I want them to do for me in Jesus name
4. May my enemies confess that my wish is their command.

Esther Chapter 6

Esther 6: 1-3, 10, 13b – On that night could not the king sleep, and he commanded to bring the book of records of the chronicles; and they were read before the king. 2 – And it was found written, that Mordecai had told of Bigthana and Teresh, two of the king's chamberlins, the keepers of the door, who sought to lay hand on the king Ahasuerus. 3 – And the king said, what honor and dignity hath been done to Mordecai for this? Then said the king's servants that ministered unto him, there is nothing done for him. 10- Then the king said to Haman, make haste, and take the apparel and the horse, as thou hast said, and do even so to Morcecai the Jew, that sitteth at the king's gate: let nothing fail of all that thou hast spoken. 13b – If Mordecai be of the seed of the Jews, before whom thou hast begun to fall, thou shalt not prevail against him, but shalt surely fall before him (KJV)

Prayer points:
1. Father, open a book of remembrance for me.
2. God, remember me and for me
3. God, use my enemies that seek my downfall to promote me in Jesus name
4. Father, may I receive the honor that is due to me in Jesus name.
5. Father, let me not fail to receive any of the promises that is due to me in Jesus name.
6. Every plan of the enemy concerning me must fail in Jesus name.
7. May my enemies surely fall before me in Jesus name Amen.
8. May my enemies not prevail against me in Jesus name. Amen.
9. May my enemies fall in the trap they have set for me in Jesus name.

Job Chapter 1

Job 1: 1 & 8 – There was a man in the land of Uz, whose name was Job; and that man was perfect and upright, and one that feared God, and eschewed evil. 8 – And the Lord said unto Satan, hast thou considered my servant Job, that there is none like him in the earth, a perfect and an upright man, one that feareth God, and escheweth evil? (KJV)

Prayer points:
1. Father, may I be perfect in Jesus name
2. Father, may I be upright in Jesus name
3. Father, may I eschew evil in Jesus name

4. Father, may your testimony concerning me be better than that of Job in Jesus name.

5. Father, may I sanctify my children continually like Job did to his children in Jesus name.

Psalm Chapter 1

Psalm 1: 1 – 6 – Blessed is the man that walketh not in the counsel of the ungodly, nor standeth in the way of sinners, nor sitteth in the seat of the scornful. 2 – But his delight is in the law of the LORD; and in his law doth he meditate day and night. 3 – And he shall be like a tree planted by the rivers of water, that bringeth forth his fruit in his season; his leaf also shall not wither; and whasoever he doeth shall prosper. 4 – The ungodly are not so: but are like the chaff which the wind driveth away. 5 – Therefore the ungodly shall not stand in judgement, nor sinners in the congregation of the righteous. 6 – For the Lord knoweth the way of the righteous: but the way of the ungodly shall perish. (KJV).

Prayer points:
1. Father, may I not walk in the counsel of the ungodly in Jesus name
2. Father, may I not stand in the way of sinners in Jesus name
3. Father, may I not sit in the seat of the scornful in Jesus name
4. May my delight be in your law, Lord in Jesus name
5. May I meditate in your word day and night in Jesus name
6. May I be like a tree planted by the rivers of water.
7. May I bring forth fruit in season
8. May I not wither in Jesus name.
9. May I prosper in whatsoever I do in Jesus name.
10. Father, may the ungodly be driven as chaff which the wind driveth away in Jesus name
11. May the ungodly not stand in the judgment, and sinners in the congregation of the righteous in Jesus name.
12. May the way of the ungodly perish in Jesus name.

Psalm Chapter 2

Prayer Points:
1. I paralize every rage of the enemy by the power in the blood of Jesus
2. Vain imagination I subdue you in Jesus name
3. Vain imagination I take you captive under the blood of Jesus
4. Vain imagination you will not stand, neither will you come to pass in Jesus name
5. Every counsel of the enemy against me and my household will not stand in Jesus name
6. Every counsel of the enemy against the children of God, you will not stand in the name of Jesus
7. Father, laugh at the enemies of your children in Jesus name
8. Let your wrath be upon the enemies of your children in Jesus name
9. Give me the heathen for my inheritance in Jesus name
10. Give me the uttermost parts of the earth for my possesion in Jesus name
11. Holy Spirit, help me to serve the Lord with fear in Jesus name
12. I shall put my trust in the Lord in Jesus name

Psalm Chapter 3

Psalm 3: 3 & 4 – But thou, O Lord, art a shield for me; my glory and the lifter up of mine head. 4 – I cried unto the Lord with my voice, and he heard me out of his holy hill. (KJV)

Prayer points:
1. Father, you are my shield
2. Father, you are my glory
3. Father, you are the lifter up of mine head
4. Father, when I cried unto you with my voice, you heard me out of your holy hill.
5. Thank you Lord for saving me

6. Thank you Lord for deliverance
7. Thank you Lord for victory
8. Thank you Lord that the enemy did not rejoice over me
9. Thank you Lord for healing

Psalm Chapter 4

Prayer Points:
1. Father, set me apart for yourself in Jesus name
2. Father, hear me when I call unto you in Jesus name
3. May I lay down in peace in Jesus name
4. May I sleep in peace without fear in Jesus name
5. Father, cause me to dwell in safety in Jesus name

Psalm Chapter 5

Prayer Points:
1. Hear me when I call on you my Father
2. Hear my thoughts oh God of heaven
3. The God to whom alone I will pray, answer my prayers in Jesus name
4. I will lift up my voice unto you early in the morning in Jesus name
5. My prayer will only be directed to you my Father
6. Remove from me all iniquity for you hate iniquity
7. Father, make thy way straight before me always in Jesus name
8. Cause my enemies to fall by their own counsel in Jesus name
9. Father, defend your children
10. Let your children rejoice in you Oh God
11. Father, compass me with favor in Jesus name
12. Father, be my shield in Jesus name.

Psalm Chapter 6

Prayer Points:
1. Father, hear my supplication in Jesus name
2. Father, hear the voice of my weeping in Jesus name
3. Father, let my prayers come unto thee in Jesus name
4. Father, receive my prayers and answer them in Jesus name
5. Let my enemies be put to shame in the name of Jesus
6. Let the shame of my enemies come to them suddenly in Jesus name

Psalm Chapter 7

Prayer Points:
1. Father you are my protector, protect me from all my persecutors in Jesus name
2. Father, you are my deliverer, deliver me from all that plan evil against me in Jesus name
3. Father you are my Savior, save me from the hands of evil men in Jesus name
4. Ordain your arrows against my persecutors in Jesus name
5. Every pit that the enemy has dug for me, let the enemy fall in the pit in Jesus name
6. Every evil plan of the enemy should return back to the enemy in Jesus name

Psalm Chapter 8

Prayer Points:
1. Excellent God, thank you for your love for me
2. Mighty God thank you for caring specially for me
3. Thank you Father for visiting me in Jesus name
4. Thank you for crowning man with glory and honor above all your creations in Jesus name

5. Thank you for the dominion that you have given me over the works of your hands in Jesus name
6. Thank you Father for the authority you have given me on earth in Jesus name
7. You are indeed a marvellous God
8. Blessed be your Holy name in Jesus name

Psalm Chapter 9

Prayer Points:
1. Father, you are the most High God
2. Father, you are the righteous judge
3. Father, you are the powerful God
4. Father, you are the judge of the whole earth
5. Father, you are the refuge for the oppressed
6. Father, you are trustworthy
7. You are the God that does not forget the cry of the humble
8. You are the merciful God
9. You are the God that lifts up
10. May my expectations never be cut off in Jesus name

Psalm Chapter 10

Prayer Points:
1. Father, do not be far from me in Jesus name
2. Father, do not hide your face from me in Jesus name
3. Every evil device that the enemy is imagining against me, return back to the enemy in Jesus name
4. Let every boast of the wicked be frustrated in Jesus name
5. Every puffing of the enemy be paralyzed in Jesus name
6. Every deceitful plan of the enemy be exposed in Jesus name
7. Father, you are the helper of the fatherless, help me oh God
8. Let the oppression of the oppressor come to an end in Jesus name

Psalm Chapter 11

Prayer Points:
1. Father in you will I put my trust in Jesus name
2. Every evil plan of the enemy against me be hindered in the name of Jesus
3. Every evil plan of the enemy againt my household be destroyed in Jesus name
4. Every evil plan of the enemy against the children of God, may it not see the light of day in Jesus name
5. Every bow of the enemy aimed at me should be broken in Jesus name
6. Every arrow the enemey has made ready for me should malfunction in Jesus name
7. Father rain snares upon the wicked in Jesus name
8. Father rain fire upon the wicked in Jesus name
9. Father rain brimstone upon the wicked in Jesus name
10. Father rain tempest upon the wicked in Jesus name
11. Let the portion of the cup of my enemies be snares in Jesus name
12. Let the portion of the cup of my enemies be fire in Jesus name
13. Let the portion of the cup of my enemies be brimstone in Jesus name
14. Let the portion of the cup of my enemies be a horrible tempest in Jesus name

Psalm Chapter 12

Prayer Points:
1. Holy Spirit take absolute control of my mouth in Jesus name
2. Grant that I will not utter vanity in Jesus name
3. May my lips not utter flattery in Jesus name
4. Father may I not speak with double heart in Jesus name
5. Remove pride from me in Jesus name
6. Remove lies from my lips in Jesus name

7. Father you are our defense, arise oh Lord and save your children
8. Arise oh Lord and fight for your children in Jesus name
9. May the vile men in our midst not be exhalted in Jesus name

Psalm Chapter 13

Prayer Points:
1. Father, please do not forget me in Jesus name
2. Father, do not hide your face from me in Jesus name
3. Father, remove sorrow from my heart in Jesus name
4. Hinder my enemies from exalting themselves over me in Jesus name
5. May I not sleep the sleep of death prematurely in Jesus name
6. May my enemies not rejoice over me in Jesus name

Psalm Chapter 14

Prayer Points:
1. May I never say in my heart that there is no God in Jesus name
2. Holy Spirit, keep me from doing abominable works in Jesus name
3. Father may I not turn away from you in Jesus name
4. When you look at me, may you not see filthiness but see the blood of Jesus that has washed me white as snow in Jesus name

Psalm Chapter 15

Prayer Points:
1. Lord, cause me to abide in your tabernacle in Jesus name
2. Holy Spirit, order my steps that my walk will be upright in Jesus name

3. Holy Spirit, order my hands that my work will be righteous in Jesus name
4. Holy Spirit, take control of my mouth that I may speak the truth in my heart in Jesus name
5. Holy Spirit, help me not to be a backbiter in Jesus name
6. Holy Spirit, help me not to do or think evil to my neighbor in Jesus name
7. May I not support the deeds of a wicked man in Jesus name
8. May I not use my money for evil in Jesus name

Psalm Chapter 16

Prayer Points:
1. May my trust be in you always oh Lord my God
2. May I not serve other gods in Jesus name
3. Father, you are my portion in Jesus name
4. I bless you my Father and my God
5. Father may I always set you before me in Jesus name
6. Because God is with me, I shall not be moved by any plan of the enemy in Jesus name
7. Father, show me continually the path of life in Jesus name
8. May I enjoy the fullness of joy in your presence in Jesus name

Psalm Chapter 17

Prayer Points:
1. Father hear me when I cry unto you in Jesus name
2. Father hear the prayer that I pray to you oh God
3. May my mouth not transgress in Jesus name
4. Direct my paths oh Lord
5. May my foot not slip in Jesus name
6. May your loving kindness not depart from me in Jesus name
7. Save me continually from those that rise up against me in Jesus name
8. May I continually be the apple of your eye oh God

9. Hide me under the shadow of your wings Father in heaven
10. Deliver me from the oppression of the wicked my Father and my God
11. Deliver me from my enemies who plan to kill me in Jesus name
12. Father let the plans of the enemy concerning me be disappointed in Jesus name
13. Deliver my soul from the wicked in Jesus name
14. Deliver my soul from wickedness in Jesus name

Psalm Chapter 18

Prayer Points:
1. Father, you are my strength
2. Father you are my fortress
3. Father you are my deliverer
4. Father you are my God
5. I will put my trust in you oh Lord
6. Father you are my buckler
7. Father you are my salvation
8. Father you are my high tower
9. Father you are worthy to be praised
10. The name of the Lord will deliver me from my enemies in Jesus name
11. Let my cry come unto you oh Lord in Jesus name
12. Father hear my cry and deliver me always in Jesus name
13. Hear my voice oh God when I call in Jesus name
14. Father deliver me from my enemies in Jesus name
15. Father deliver me from those that are too strong for me in Jesus name
16. May I not depart from your presence oh Lord
17. May I keep your commandments oh Lord
18. Keep me Father from iniquity in Jesus name
19. Father show me your mercy in Jesus name
20. Father save me from affliction of the enemy in Jesus name

21. Father let your light shine in my darkness in Jesus name
22. Help me oh God by the power in the blood of Jesus to run through the enemies that are in my way in Jesus name
23. Help me oh God by the power in the blood of Jesus to leap over every barrier and hindrances the enemy has put in my way in Jesus name
24. Father your way is the perfect way
25. Father you are my rock
26. Father teach my hands to war so that I can break a bow of steel with my hands in Jesus name
27. Father do the miraculous in my life in Jesus name
28. Father do the wonderful in my life in Jesus name
29. May I not turn back from pursuing my enemies until they are destroyed in Jesus name
30. May my enemies not be able to rise up against me forevermore in Jesus name
31. Father guard me with divine strength in Jesus name
32. Let my enemies be continually under my feet in Jesus name
33. Give me the necks of my enemies continually in Jesus name
34. Give me the strength to beat my enemies small as the dust before the wind in Jesus name
35. Cause me to cast sickness, disease, infirmity out of my life as the dirt in the streets in Jesus name
36. Make me the head oh God and not the tail in Jesus name
37. Let the people who I do not know serve me in Jesus name
38. Let the words that come out of my mouth come with authority, that as soon as my enemies hear it they will obey in Jesus name
39. Wickedness shall bow before me in Jesus name
40. Let every plant that you have not planted in me fade away in Jesus name
41. Let every plant that you have not planted in me be afraid to remain in me in Jesus name
42. May your name be exalted oh God now and forevermore in Jesus name

43. Father you are the avenger, avenge me of my enemies in Jesus name
44. Subdue every evil plan of the enemy under my feet in Jesus name
45. Father deliver me from my enemies in Jesus name
46. Father lift me up above those who rise up against me in Jesus name
47. Father deliver me from the violent man in Jesus name
48. Father I thank you for your mercy
49. Father I thank you for your love
50. I thank you oh God for your protection
51. Lord God I thank you for your provision
52. Thank you Jesus

Psalm Chapter 19

Prayer Points:
1. Father let the heavens declare your glory in Jesus name
2. Let the firmament show forth your beautiful work in Jesus name
3. Father you are the mighty God
4. Father you are the powerful God
5. Nothing can hide from your heat
6. Nothing can hide from your cold
7. Nothing can hide from your light
8. Father fearing you is the beginning of wisdom
9. Father you are a righteous judge
10. Clean me from secret faults oh Lord my God
11. Keep me from sins of presumption in Jesus name
12. Let sin not have dominion over me in Jesus name
13. Father let the words that I speak be right in your ears oh God in Jesus name
14. Father let the meditations of my heart be right before you oh my Father in Jesus name

15. Let my life as a whole be acceptable in your sight oh Lord my God in Jesus name
16. Father you are my strength
17. Father you are my redeemer

Psalm Chapter 20

Prayer Points:
1. Father when I call upon you in the day of trouble hear me in Jesus name
2. Father let your name defend me in Jesus name
3. My help is in you oh Lord
4. Father you are my strength
5. Father remember my offerings oh Lord
6. Father accept my sacrifice of praise in Jesus name
7. Father accept my sacrifice of thanksgiving in Jesus name
8. Father accept my sacrifice of worship in Jesus name
9. Father grant the request of my heart in accordance to your perfect will for my life in Jesus name

Psalm Chapter 21

Prayer Points:
1. Father grant my heart's desire in accordance to your perfect will for my life in Jesus name
2. Father may I not die prematurely in Jesus name
3. May I live to good old age in Jesus name
4. Father bless me forever in Jesus name
5. Father make me a blessing in Jesus name
6. Give me joy in my heart oh God in Jesus name
7. May my enemies not be hid from me in Jesus name
8. May those that hate me not be hid from me in Jesus name
9. Let every net the enemy has set for me catch the enemy
10. Let the enemy fall in the pit that they dig for me in Jesus name

11. May the enemy not be able to perform their mischief against me in Jesus name
12. Be thou exalted oh Lord my God

Psalm Chapter 22

Prayer Points:
1. Father do not forsake me in Jesus name
2. Father do not be far from me in Jesus name
3. Father hear my cry and answer me in Jesus name
4. Whenever I cry, Lord hear and answer me in Jesus name
5. Father inhabit my praise as I begin to praise you in Jesus name
6. Father deliver me oh God in Jesus name
7. Father I will always trust you in Jesus name
8. Permit no man to laugh at me in Jesus name
9. Father do not be far from me in Jesus name
10. You are my Creator
11. Your are my help
12. Strengthen me oh Lord before my enemies in Jesus name
13. Give me boldness when I am face to face with my enemies in Jesus name
14. Father you are my deliverer, deliver my soul from the enemy in Jesus name

Psalm Chapter 23

Prayer Points:
1. Father because you are my shepherd, I will not lack anything good in Jesus name
2. Father because you are my shepherd, perfect health is my portion in Jesus name
3. Father because you are my shepherd, perfect peace is my portion in Jesus name

4. Father because you are my shepherd, joy is my portion in Jesus name
5. Father because you are my shepherd, I shall have all I set my heart to have in accordance to your will in Jesus name
6. Father your Holy Spirit will lead me through the righteous path just because of your Holy name in Jesus name
7. Even when there are troubles around me, I will not be afraid because you are my shepherd
8. I know that you are with me always, therefore I will not be afraid in Jesus name
9. My comfort is from you oh God and not from man
10. Father prepare a table before me in the presence of my enemies in Jesus name
11. Let the enemy see and know that I serve the living God in Jesus name
12. Let the enemy see and know that I serve a mighty God in Jesus name
13. Let the enemy see and know that I serve the Creator of heaven and earth
14. Bless me abundantly oh Lord my God
15. May I be a blessing oh Lord my God in Jesus name
16. Let goodness follow me all the days of my life in Jesus name
17. Let mercy follow me all the days of my life in Jesus name
18. May I not depart from your presence oh Lord my God in Jesus name

Psalm Chapter 24

Prayer Points:
1. Father you are the Creator of heaven and earth
2. Holy Spirit cleanse my hands that I will be worthy to ascend into the hill of the Lord in Jesus name
3. Holy Spirit cleanse my heart, that I may be able to ascend into the hill of the Lord in Jesus name
4. Father forgive me of any vanity in Jesus name

5. Father forgive me of any deceitful swearing in Jesus name
6. Father you are the King of glory
7. Father you are strong
8. Father you are the mighty God
9. Father you are the Lord of Hosts

Psalm Chapter 25

Prayer Points:
1. Father you are the only one I will lift up my voice to in Jesus name
2. Father may I not be put to shame in Jesus name because they that put their trust in you shall not be put to shame
3. Father do not permit my enemies to have victory over me in Jesus name
4. Holy Spirit lead me in the truth
5. Father sanctify me in thy word, because thy word is true
6. Father forgive all my tresspasses in Jesus name
7. Father you are good
8. Father your are upright
9. Father cause my soul to dwell at ease in Jesus name
10. Cause my seed to inherit the earth in Jesus name

Psalm Chapter 26

Prayer Points:
1. Father may my trust be in you continually in Jesus name
2. Father may I not slide away from you in Jesus name
3. May I not sit with vain persons in Jesus name
4. May I not associate with dissemblers in Jesus name

Psalm Chapter 27

Prayer Points:
1. Lord you are my light

2. Lord you are my salvation
3. I will not fear any man in Jesus name
4. Lord you are the strength of my life
5. My enemies will stumble in Jesus name
6. Father may I seek you all the days of my life in Jesus name
7. Father may I dwell in your presence all the days of my life in Jesus name
8. Father may I see your beauty all the days of my life in Jesus name
9. Father hide me in your pavillion in the day of trouble in Jesus name
10. Father set me up upon a solid rock in Jesus name
11. Father I will sing praises to your Holy name in Jesus name
12. Hear my cry oh Lord when I cry in Jesus name
13. May your mercy towards me never cease in Jesus name
14. Never hide your face from me Lord in Jesus name
15. Do not be angry with me oh Lord in Jesus name
16. Do not leave me oh Lord in Jesus name
17. Do not forsake me oh Lord in Jesus name
18. God you are my salvation
19. I will see the goodness of the Lord in the land of the living in Jesus name
20. Father strengthen my heart in Jesus name

Psalm Chapter 28

Prayer Points:
1. I cry unto you oh God of heaven in the name of Jesus
2. Father hear my cry and do not be silent in Jesus name
3. Do not allow me to go the way of the wicked oh Lord in Jesus name
4. Father you are my strength in Jesus name
5. Father you are my salvation in Jesus name
6. Father you are my shield in Jesus name
7. Father you are my help in Jesus name

8. Lord my heart will trust in you continually in Jesus name
9. Father bless me forever in Jesus name
10. Father lift me up forever in Jesus name

Psalm Chapter 29

Prayer Points:
1. Father I give you glory for you deserve all the glory
2. Father I ascribe strength unto you for you are worthy
3. Father I worship you for there is none like you in all the earth
4. Father your voice is powerful
5. Father your voice is full of majesty
6. Father your voice can break what needs to be broken
7. Father your voice can mend what needs to be mended
8. Father your voice can divide fires
9. Father your voice can shake the wilderness
10. Father you are king forevermore
11. Father give me strength in Jesus name
12. Father give me peace in Jesus name

Psalm Chapter 30

Prayer Points:
1. I exalt you oh Lord for you are the lifter up of my head
2. I exalt you oh Lord for you have not allowed my enemies to rejoice over me
3. I exalt you oh Lord for healing me in Jesus name
4. I exalt you oh Lord for the gift of life in Jesus name
5. Father make my mountain to stand strong in Jesus name
6. Have mercy upon me oh Lord my helper in Jesus name
7. Father turn for me my mourning into dancing in Jesus name
8. I remove the sack cloth off my body in Jesus name
9. I put on the garment of gladness in Jesus name

Psalm Chapter 31

Prayer Points:
1. I will put my trust in you oh Lord
2. Father may I never be put to shame
3. Your word says that they that put their trust in the Lord shall never be ashamed, therefore I shall never be ashamed for my trust is in the Lord in Jesus name
4. Father I declare that you are my deliverer in Jesus name
5. Father I declare that you are my strong rock therefore I shall not be moved in Jesus name
6. Father I declare that you are my Savior in Jesus name
7. Father I declare that you are my fortress in Jesus name
8. Father I declare that you are my leader in Jesus name
9. Father I declare that you are my guide in Jesus name
10. Father I declare that you are my strength in Jesus name
11. Father your word says that as you hear me speak so will you do, do according to all that I have spoken in Jesus name
12. Father deliver me from every net the enemy has set for me in Jesus name
13. Father let the enemy be caught in the net they have set for me in Jesus name
14. Father you are my Redeemer
15. You are the God of truth and your word is true, therefore, sanctify me by your word which is true in Jesus name
16. May I hate the lies of liars in Jesus name
17. May my life not be consumed in grief in Jesus name
18. May my years not be filled with sighing in Jesus name
19. Forgive all my iniquities and the ability to commit iniquity in Jesus name
20. May I not be a reproach among all my enemies in Jesus name
21. May I not fear anyone but the Lord God Almighty in Jesus name
22. Every counsel of the enemy against me be destroyed by the fire of God in Jesus name

23. Every devise of the enemy to take my life should backfire in Jesus name
24. Father my trust will forever be in you for you are my God in Jesus name
25. Father deliver me from my enemies in Jesus name
26. Father deliver me from my persecutors in Jesus name
27. May your face shine upon me continually in Jesus name
28. May I never be put to shame in Jesus name
29. Let the wicked be put to shame in Jesus name
30. Let the lying lips be shut up in Jesus name
31. Thank you Father for laying up goodness for those who fear you in Jesus name
32. Thank you Father for your kindness in Jesus name
33. Thank you for preserving the faithful in Jesus name

Psalm Chapter 32

Prayer Points:
1. Father forgive my transgressions in Jesus name
2. Father may there not be any devious way in me so that I will be blessed in Jesus name
3. Father let not your hands be heavy upon me in Jesus name
4. Father may I always acknowledge my sins in Jesus name
5. May I not hide my iniquities in Jesus name
6. I will confess all my sins to you Lord for cleansing because you are the one that cleanses from all unrighteousness
7. Father I will seek you when you can be found in Jesus name
8. Father you are my hiding place
9. You are my preserver – preserve me from all troubles in Jesus name
10. Father you are my deliverer – deliver me from my enemies in Jesus name
11. Let your Holy Spirit instruct me in the way I should go daily in Jesus name
12. Let your Holy Spirit guide my steps daily in Jesus name

13. Let your mercy surround me everyday of my life in Jesus name
14. I will rejoice in you oh Lord
15. I will be glad in you oh Lord
16. I will make a joyful shout unto you oh Lord

Psalm Chapter 33

Prayer Points:
1. Father I believe that your word is right in Jesus name
2. Father I believe that your works are true
3. Father you are the God that loves righteousness
4. Father the earth is full of your goodness
5. Father by the words of your mouth you created the heavens and the earth
6. Father by the breath of your mouth you made man a living being
7. There is none like you in all the earth
8. Father you are the God that can make the counsel of the wicked to become foolishness
9. Father you are the God that can hinder the plans of the wicked
10. Father you are a great God that can see all the earth from your throne in Heaven
11. Father you are my shield
12. Father you are my hope
13. Father you are my help
14. Have mercy upon me oh God

Psalm Chapter 34

Prayer Points:
1. Holy Spirit cause me to bless the Lord at all times
2. Holy Spirit cause the praise of the Lord to be on my lips at all times in Jesus name

3. Holy Spirit cause me not to be ashamed of the name of the Lord, but to make boast of the name of the Lord
4. Father you are the Lord that delivered me from all my troubles, blessed be your Holy name
5. Father you are the merciful God that hears the cry of the poor
6. Father you are the merciful God that delivers the poor from all their trouble – to you be glory, honor and praise in Jesus name
7. Father cause your angel to encamp round about me in Jesus name
8. Holy Spirit, take control of my tongue that I will not utter evil in Jesus name
9. Help me Lord to seek peace and to pursue it in Jesus name
10. Father let your eyes be upon me all the days of my life in Jesus name
11. Father hear me when I call in Jesus name
12. Father keep all my bones, let none be broken in Jesus name

Psalm Chapter 35

Prayer Points:
1. Father fight against them that fight against me in Jesus name
2. Let everyone that seek after my soul for evil be put to shame in Jesus name
3. Send confusion into the camp of my enemies in Jesus name
4. Let my enemies begin to run even when no one is chasing them in Jesus name
5. Let the paths of my enemies be dark in Jesus name
6. Let the ways of my enemies be slippery in Jesus name
7. Let destruction come upon my enemies suddenly in Jesus name
8. Let every net that the enemy has set for me catch my enemies in Jesus name
9. Father do not let my enemies rejoice over me in Jesus name
10. Father bless those that bless me in Jesus name
11. Father curse those that curse me in Jesus name

Psalm Chapter 36

Prayer Points:
1. Father may the words of my mouth not be words of iniquity in Jesus name
2. Father may the words of my mouth not be deceitful words in Jesus name
3. May I not devise mischief upon my bed in Jesus name
4. May I pursue after righteousness in Jesus name
5. Satisfy me oh Lord with your presence in Jesus name
6. Make me drink of the river of your pleasures oh Lord in Jesus name
7. Father protect me from the foot of pride in Jesus name
8. Father deliver me from the hand of the wicked in Jesus name

Psalm Chapter 37

Prayer Points:
1. I will not be envious of workers of iniquity in Jesus name
2. I will delight myself in the Lord in Jesus name
3. Father grant me the desires of my heart in accordance to your perfect will for my life in Jesus name
4. Spirit of impatience I come against you in Jesus name
5. Deliver me oh Lord from anger in Jesus name
6. Let the spirit that is in my Lord Jesus Christ make a permanent habitation in me in Jesus name
7. Spirit of meekness, I welcome you into my life in Jesus name
8. Let the sword that the wicked has prepared for me enter into their hearts in Jesus name
9. Father break the arms of the wicked in Jesus name
10. Father satisfiy my soul in the days of famine in Jesus name
11. Father order my steps in Jesus name
12. Father take delight in my ways in Jesus name
13. When I fall, I will not be utterly cast down because the Lord will hold me with His hand in Jesus name

14. The Lord will not forsake me in Jesus name
15. I will not beg for bread in Jesus name
16. My seed will not beg for bread in Jesus name
17. May my mouth speak wisdom in Jesus name
18. Father may your law be in my heart that none of my steps shall slide in Jesus name
19. Father may my end be peaceful in Jesus name
20. Father you are my strength in time of trouble
21. Father my trust is in you
22. Deliver me from the hand of the wicked in Jesus name

Psalm Chapter 38

Prayer Points:
1. Father do not scold me when you are extrememly angry with me in Jesus name
2. Father do not punish me when you are not all happy with me in Jesus name
3. Father my hope is in you all day long in Jesus name
4. Do not allow the enemies to rejoice over me in Jesus name
5. Father forgive all my sins in Jesus name
6. Grant that I will follow what is good regardless of what the world is doing in Jesus name
7. Help me o Lord my savior in Jesus name

Psalm Chapter 39

Prayer Points:
1. Holy Spirit, take total control of my tongue that I will not sin in Jesus name
2. May my focus in life not be to heap up riches in Jesus name
3. May my hope be in you continually and not in riches in Jesus name
4. Father hear my prayer oh Lord God in Jesus name

Psalm Chapter 40

Prayer Points:
1. I receive the spirit of patience in Jesus name
2. Father deliver me from the pit and set my feet upon the solid rock in Jesus name
3. Father put a new song in my mouth in Jesus name
4. Father put a song of praise unto your Holy name in my mouth in Jesus name
5. May my trust be in you continually in Jesus name
6. May I never turn to lies in Jesus name
7. Father great are the works of your hands
8. Father may I do your will all the days of my life in Jesus name
9. Help me Holy Spirit to declare God's faithfulness in Jesus name
10. Help me Holy Spirit to declare God's righteousness in Jesus name
11. May your goodness and mercy follow me all the days of my life in Jesus name
12. Father deliver me from every trouble in Jesus name
13. Father confuse every gathering of my enemies in Jesus name
14. Father bring to shame those that seek evil for me in Jesus name
15. Lord be magnified
16. Lord you are my help
17. Lord you are my deliverer

Psalm Chapter 41

Prayer Points:
1. Father deliver me in time of trouble in Jesus name
2. Father preserve me oh Lord in Jesus name
3. Father keep me alive in Jesus name
4. Father bless me in Jesus name
5. Father strengthen me in Jesus name

6. Father be merciful unto me in Jesus name
7. Father heal my soul in Jesus name
8. Father frustrate the desires of my enemies in Jesus name
9. Father do not allow my enemies to triumph over me in Jesus name

Psalm Chapter 42

Prayer Points:
1. Father cause my soul to pant after you in Jesus name
2. My soul shall not be quiet but I shall hope in God and praise God in Jesus name
3. Father command your loving kindness upon me in the daytime in Jesus name
4. Father may your song of praise and prayer not depart from my mouth at night in Jesus name
5. Father please do not forget me in Jesus name
6. Father you are my health

Psalm Chapter 43

Prayer Points:
1. Father deliver me from the deceitful and the unjust in Jesus name
2. God you are my strength
3. Do not cast me off oh Lord my God
4. Lead me by your light oh Lord in Jesus name
5. Lead me by your truth oh Lord in Jesus name
6. Father you are my exceeding joy

Psalm Chapter 44

Prayer Points:
1. Father drive out my enemies from before me in Jesus name
2. Father plant my feet upon the solid ground in Jesus name

3. Father afflict those that afflict me in Jesus name
4. My trust is in you oh God
5. Do not turn back from me oh God in Jesus name
6. Father may my steps not decline from your way oh God in Jesus name
7. Father forgive me of all my trespasses in Jesus name
8. Father deliver me for your name sake in Jesus name

Psalm Chapter 45

Prayer Points:
1. Bless me for ever oh God in Jesus name
2. Let your arrows be sharp in the heart of my enemies oh God in Jesus name

Psalm Chapter 46

Prayer Points:
1. God you are my refuge
2. God you are my strength
3. Father you are a present help in time of trouble
4. Father because you are my God, I shall not be moved in Jesus name
5. The Lord of hosts is with me
6. The God of Jacob is my refuge in Jesus name
7. Be thou exalted our God in the earth in Jesus name

Psalm Chapter 47

Prayer Points:
1. Father you are the king over all the earth
2. I will praise your name forever
3. I exalt you my God

Psalm Chapter 48

Prayer Points:
1. Father you are a great God
2. Father you deserve the praise and glory
3. You are beautiful for every situation
4. You are the joy of the whole earth
5. God you are my God
6. God you will forever be my guide from now and unto the end in Jesus name

Psalm Chapter 49

Prayer Points:
1. Father deliver me from foolishness in Jesus name
2. Father deliver my soul from the power of the grave in Jesus name
3. Father give me understanding in Jesus name

Psalm Chapter 50

Prayer Points:
1. Father you are the righteous judge
2. Father the earth and the fullness of it belongs to you
3. I will offer unto you thanksgiving in Jesus name
4. I will pay my vows unto you oh God in Jesus name
5. I will call upon you oh God in the day of trouble for deliverance in Jesus name
6. I will glorify your holy name oh God
7. I will not hate instruction
8. I will not company with a thief in Jesus name
9. I will not give myself to evil in Jesus name
10. I will not give my tongue to deceit in Jesus name
11. Holy Spirit take control of my mouth that I may not speak evil against my brethren in Jesus name

12. Holy Spirit take control of my mouth that I may not slander my brethren in Jesus name
13. Father I will glorify you with my praise in Jesus name
14. I will order my conversation aright that I may see the salvation of my God in Jesus name

Psalm Chapter 51

Prayer Points:
1. Have mercy upon me oh God
2. Cleanse me from all my transgressions oh God
3. Father make me to hear joy and gladness in Jesus name
4. Create in me a clean heart oh God
5. Renew a right spirit with me oh God
6. Do not cast me away from your presence God
7. Do not take your Holy Spirit from me oh God
8. Restore unto me the joy of your salvation oh God
9. Deliver me from bloodguiltiness oh God in Jesus name
10. May my lips sing your praise oh God in Jesus name

Psalm Chapter 52

Prayer Points:
1. Spirit behind boasting I cast you out of my life in Jesus name
2. Spirit behind mischiefs I cast you out of my life in Jesus name
3. Spirit behind deceit I cast you out of my life in Jesus name
4. God help me to love good more than evil in Jesus name
5. God help me to love righteousness rather than to speak lies in Jesus name
6. I will make God my strength in Jesus name
7. I will not trust in riches in Jesus name
8. I shall be like a green olive tree in the house of God forever in Jesus name
9. I shall trust in God's mercy all the days of my life in Jesus name

Psalm Chapter 53

Prayer Points:
1. I refuse to be a fool in Jesus name
2. I know, I believe and I confess that there is a God in Jesus name
3. Father deliver me from captivity in Jesus name

Psalm Chapter 54

Prayer Points:
1. The name of the Lord save me
2. The name of the Lord deliver me
3. The name of the Lord heal me
4. The name of the Lord promote me
5. The name of the Lord comfort me
6. The name of the Lord uphold me
7. Hear my prayer oh God
8. Lord you are my helper

Psalm Chapter 55

Prayer Points:
1. Hear me oh God when I call because of my enemies in Jesus name
2. Deliver me from the spirit of fear in Jesus name
3. Father destroy the tongues of my enemies in Jesus name
4. Father divide the tongues of my enemies in Jesus name
5. Father may I not cause distress for my brethren in Jesus name
6. Father may my brethren not cause me distress in Jesus name
7. Deliver me oh God from the battle that is against me in Jesus name
8. May I not be moved because of my enemies in Jesus name

Psalm Chapter 56

Prayer Points:

1. Have mercy upon me oh God
2. Deliver me from being swallowed up by man that fights me daily in Jesus name
3. Lord I put my trust in you and I will not fear what man can do to me in Jesus name
4. Father do not allow the evil immaginations of my enemies to come to pass in Jesus name
5. Scatter the gathering of my enemies in Jesus name
6. Send confusion into the camp of my enemies in Jesus name
7. Father deliver my feet from falling in Jesus name
8. Cause me to walk before you oh God in the light of the living in Jesus name

Psalm Chapter 57

Prayer Points:

1. Have mercy upon me Oh God
2. I put my trust in you oh God
3. Father you are my refuge
4. You are the God that performs all things for me, therefore I will cry unto you in Jesus name
5. Father save me from the reproach of man in Jesus name
6. Be thou exalted oh God above the heavens in Jesus name
7. Father let your glory be above all the earth in Jesus name
8. Cause my enemies to fall into the pit they have dug for me in Jesus name
9. Father cause my enemies to be caught by the net they have hid for me in Jesus name
10. I will awake early and sing praise to my God
11. I will sing the praise of God wherever I go in Jesus name
12. Be thou exalted oh God above the heavens, let your glory be above all the earth

Psalm Chapter 58

Prayer Points:
1. Father break the teeth of the wicked in their mouth in Jesus name
2. Let my enemies melt away as waters which run continually in Jesus name
3. Cut into pieces the bows of my enemies in Jesus name
4. Let my enemies pass away as untimely birth of a woman in Jesus name
5. Let every evil plan of my enemies not see the light of day in the name of Jesus name
6. Father you are the great judge

Psalm Chapter 59

Prayer Points:
1. Father deliver and defend me from my enemies in Jesus name
2. Father laugh at my enemies in derision
3. Father cause my desires on my enemies to come to pass in Jesus name
4. Lord you are my shield
5. God you are the powerful God
6. Father you are the merciful God

Psalm Chapter 60

Prayer Points:
1. Father forgive our nation of our sins oh God in Jesus name
2. Father heal our land oh God in Jesus name

Psalm Chapter 61

Prayer Points:
1. Hear my cry oh God and save me in Jesus name

2. Holy Spirit lead me to the rock that is higher than I in Jesus name
3. Father you are my shelter
4. Father you are my strong tower

Psalm Chapter 62

Prayer Points:
1. God you are my salvation
2. God you are my rock
3. God you are my defense therefore I shall not be moved in Jesus name
4. May I not bless with my mouth and curse inwardly in Jesus name
5. My expectation is from God, therefore I will wait on God and not on man in Jesus name
6. God you are my refuge
7. I will put my trust in God at all times
8. I will pour out my heart unto God in Jesus name
9. Once has God spoken, twice have I heard that power belongs to God

Psalm Chapter 63

Prayer Points:
1. God you are my God
2. Early in the morning I will seek your face
3. My soul thirsts for God
4. My flesh longs for God
5. Your loving kindness is better than life
6. My lips shall praise you oh Lord
7. I will lift up my hands in your name
8. My mouth shall praise your holy name
9. I will remember you when I am upon my bed

10. I will meditate on your faithfulness, your power, your might, your mercy, your favor in the night
11. Father you have been my help therefore I will rejoice in you and be glad
12. The desires of the enemy concerning me will not come to pass in Jesus name
13. Father stop the mouth of the wicked in Jesus name

Psalm Chapter 64

Prayer Points:
1. Remove every fear of the enemy from me oh Lord in Jesus name
2. Hide me from the secret counsel of the enemy oh Lord in Jesus name
3. Every arrow of the wicked fashioned against me I command you to backfire in Jesus name
4. Father shoot your arrow at my enemies in Jesus name
5. Let all the upright glory in you oh God
6. Give gladness to the righteous oh God in Jesus name

Psalm Chapter 65

Prayer Points:
1. Father purge away my transgression in Jesus name
2. Father cause me to dwell in your court in Jesus name
3. You are the God of my salvation
4. Father you are my confidence in Jesus name
5. You are the mighty God
6. Great are your works oh Lord my God

Psalm Chapter 66

Prayer Points:
1. Father in heaven, I will make a joyful noise unto you in the name of Jesus
2. I will sing of your honor, I will make your praise known in Jesus name
3. You are the powerful God in whom all your enemies have no choice but to submit
4. The whole earth shall worship you because of your greatness
5. You are the God that has absolute control over nature itself
6. You are the breath that I breathe
7. You are the life that I live
8. Nothing is too difficult for you o Lord my God
9. You are the God of all the earth
10. Holy Spirit remove every wickedness from me so that the Lord can hear me in Jesus name
11. Father hear me when I call in Jesus name
12. Father do not turn away your mercy from me in Jesus name

Psalm Chapter 67

Prayer Points:
1. Father be merciful to us in Jesus name
2. Father bless us in Jesus name
3. Father cause your face to shine upon us in Jesus name
4. Father put your praise in our mouths in Jesus name

Psalm Chapter 68

Prayer Points:
1. God arise and let all your enemies be scattered in Jesus name
2. At the mention of the name of Jesus, let all our enemies flee in Jesus name
3. Give your children joy oh Lord in Jesus name

4. Almighty Father you are the father of the fatherless
5. Almighty God, you are the husband of the widow
6. You are the help of the helpless
7. You are the hope of the hopeless
8. You are the healer of the sick
9. You are the companion of the lonely
10. You are the deliverer of the oppressed
11. Thank you Lord for daily loading me with benefits in Jesus name
12. You are the God of my salvation
13. God be praise now and forevermore

Psalm Chapter 69

Prayer Points:
1. Save me oh God for you are my savior in Jesus name
2. Deliver me from those that hate me without a cause in Jesus name
3. I will not be ashamed because your words says that they that put their trust in you shall not be put to shame in Jesus name
4. May my prayer be unto you oh Lord my God in Jesus name
5. Hear my prayers oh Lord and deliver me from my enemies in Jesus name
6. Father deliver me even from those that hate me in Jesus name
7. Do not let the waterflood overflow me in Jesus name
8. Permit not the deep to swallow me in Jesus name
9. Do not let the pit shut her mouth upon me in Jesus name
10. May I receive your mercy in Jesus name
11. When I am in trouble, Lord do not hide your face from me in Jesus name
12. Father do not delay in answering me in Jesus name
13. May I not beg for pity from man in Jesus name
14. May I not seek comforters among men in Jesus name
15. Holy Spirit I declare you my comforter in Jesus name

16. Let the table of my enemies become a snare for them in Jesus name
17. Anything that should have been for the welfare of my enemies should be a trap in Jesus name
18. Cause their eyes to be darkened that they see not in Jesus name
19. Make their loins shake continually in Jesus name
20. Pour out your anger upon my enemies in Jesus name

Psalm Chapter 70

Prayer Points:
1. Deliver me oh God for you are my deliverer
2. Help me oh God for you are my helper
3. Bring shame upon those that seek after my soul in Jesus name
4. Bring sudden confusion upon those that seek after my soul in Jesus name
5. Let the children of God say continually, God be magnified

Psalm Chapter 71

Prayer Points:
1. My trust is in you oh Lord
2. Remove every confusion from me oh Lord
3. Deliver me oh Lord
4. Save me oh Lord
5. Be my strong habitation continually oh Lord
6. Father you are my rock
7. Father you are my fortress
8. Father you are my hope
9. I will praise you now and forevermore
10. You are my strong refuge oh Lord
11. I will sing your praise all day long
12. I will honor your Holy Name all day long

13. Father disappoint everyone that desires evil for me in Jesus name
14. Father cause me to tell of your greatness to this generation and the one to come in Jesus name
15. Father you are the great God
16. Father there is none like you in all the earth
17. Father increase my greatness in Jesus name
18. Father comfort me on every side in Jesus name

Psalm Chapter 72

Prayer Points:
1. Father you are the righteous judge
2. Father save your children in Jesus name
3. Father cause the righteous to flourish in Jesus name
4. You are the God that does wondrous things

Psalm Chapter 73

Prayer Points:
1. Holy Spirit remove foolishness from me that I will not be envious of the prosperity of the wicked in Jesus name
2. Holy Spirit remove pride from me in Jesus name
3. Holy Spirit remove wickedness from me in Jesus name
4. Father hold me continually by my right hand in Jesus name
5. Holy Spirit guide me by counsel in Jesus name
6. Father you are the one that I have in heaven
7. Cause my desire upon this earth to be for you oh Lord in Jesus name
8. Father you are my strength in Jesus name
9. Father you are my portion now and forever in Jesus name

Psalm Chapter 74

Prayer Points:
1. Father do not cast us off from your presence oh Lord
2. Hinder the enemies that have come in our midst to destroy the works of your hands oh Lord
3. Father forgive us our iniquities and raise among us prophets oh Lord

Psalm Chapter 75

Prayer Points:
1. I give you thanks my Father in heaven
2. Promote me oh Lord because promotion comes from you
3. Father put down every wickedness in me in Jesus name
4. Father put down every pride in me in Jesus name
5. Father I pray for the spirit of humility in Jesus name
6. Father I pray for a meek spirit in Jesus name
7. Father cut off the horns of the wicked in Jesus name
8. Father exalt the horn of the righteous in Jesus name

Psalm Chapter 76

Prayer Points:
1. Father you are the powerful God
2. Father you are the mighty God
3. None in all the earth can withstand you

Psalm Chapter 77

Prayer Points:
1. Father thank you for hearing my cry unto you in Jesus name
2. Father do not shut up your mercies in your anger in Jesus name
3. Father you are a wonder working God

4. I will meditate on your goodness, your power and your might in Jesus name

Psalm Chapter 78

Prayer Points:
1. Holy Spirit help me to make known God's commandment to my children.
2. May my children know your commandments oh God
3. May my children obey your commandment oh God
4. May my children teach your commandments oh God
5. May my children observe your commandments oh God
6. May my children's hope be in you oh God
7. May my children not forget your works oh God
8. May my children keep your commandment oh God
9. May my children not be a stubborn generation
10. May my children not be a rebellious generation
11. May my children not be a generation that does not set their hearts aright
12. May my children not be counted among those whose spirit is not steadfast
13. Father anything that represents the Red Sea in my life be divided
14. Cause me to pass through every obstacle on my way
15. Father lead me in the day time with a cloud
16. Father lead me all night with a light of fire
17. Cause me to prosper even in times of famine
18. Father may I not provoke you to anger
19. Father may I not tempt you in my heart
20. May I not speak against you
21. May my days not be consumed in vanity
22. May my years not be consumed in trouble
23. Father I confess you are my rock
24. Lord I confess you are my redeemer

25. I will not flatter you with my mouth
26. I will not lie to you with my tongue
27. Holy Spirit direct my heart to always be right with God
28. Father may I not limit you

Psalm Chapter 79

Prayer Points:
1. Father deliver us from the oppression of our enemies in Jesus name
2. Father do not allow the enemy to rejoice over us in Jesus name
3. Forgive us oh God our iniquities in Jesus name
4. Help us our Father and our God in Jesus name
5. Have mercy upon us oh God in Jesus name

Psalm Chapter 80

Prayer Points:
1. Father you are our sherpherd, guide us in Jesus name
2. Father you are our leader, lead us in Jesus name
3. Father you are our savior, save us in Jesus name
4. Do not allow the enemy to laugh at us in Jesus name

Psalm Chapter 81

Prayer Points:
1. Father you are worthy to be praised
2. When I called in trouble, you delivered me
3. You are the God my deliverer
4. Holy Spirit cause me to walk in the counsel of the almighty God in Jesus name
5. Holy Spirit help me to do the will of God in Jesus name
6. Father subdue my enemies in Jesus name
7. Lord turn your hands against my adversaries in Jesus name

Psalm Chapter 82

Prayer Points:
1. Father defend me oh God in Jesus name
2. Deliver me from the hand of the wicked in Jesus name

Psalm Chapter 83

Prayer Points:
1. Fight with them that fight against me oh God
2. Contend with them that contend with me oh God
3. Defend me oh God
4. Father bring shame upon my enemies in Jesus name
5. Bring trouble upon my enemies oh God

Psalm Chapter 84

Prayer Points:
1. My strength is in thee oh Lord
2. Your ways are in my heart oh Lord
3. May I go from strength to strength oh Lord
4. May I be a blessing wherever I go in Jesus name
5. May I appear before you daily with thanksgiving and praise in Jesus name
6. I will trust in the Lord my God
7. I will walk uprightly in Jesus name
8. Father do not withhold any good thing from me in Jesus name

Psalm Chapter 85

Prayer Points:
1. Thank you Father for forgiving my iniquities in Jesus name
2. Father revive me again oh Lord in Jesus name
3. Show me your mercy oh God in Jesus name
4. Father speak peace unto me in Jesus name

Psalm Chapter 86

Prayer Points:
1. Hear my cry oh Lord
2. Save me oh Lord in Jesus name
3. Have mercy upon me Lord God of heaven and earth
4. Give me joy in my heart of Lord
5. You are a merciful God

Psalm Chapter 87

Prayer Points:
1. Lord establish me in Jesus name
2. Set my feet upon Christ the solid rock in Jesus name

Psalm Chapter 88

Prayer Points:
1. Father let my prayer come to thee in Jesus name
2. Father incline your ears unto me in Jesus name
3. Deliver me from premature death in Jesus name

Psalm Chapter 89

Prayer Points:
1. Father I will sing of your mercies all the days of my life in Jesus name
2. Father I will tell of your faithfulness in Jesus name
3. There is none that can be compared with thee oh Lord
4. You are the almighty God
5. You are the maker of heaven and earth
6. Father save and deliver my children and I with your mighty arm, for strong is your hand and high is your right hand
7. Father you are our strength in Jesus name
8. Father you are our defense

9. You are our king
10. May the enemy not exact upon me in Jesus name
11. May the son of wickedness not afflict me in Jesus name
12. Father beat down my foes before my face in Jesus name
13. Father like you did to Egypt, plague them that hate me in Jesus name

Psalm Chapter 90

Prayer Points:
1. Lord you are my dwelling place
2. Father teach me to number my days in Jesus name
3. Help me Holy Spirit to apply my heart to wisdom in Jesus name
4. Father let your beauty be upon me in Jesus name
5. Father establish the works of my hands in Jesus name

Psalm Chapter 91

Prayer Points:
1. Lord you are my refuge
2. Lord you are my trust
3. Lord you my fortress
4. Lord you are my deliverer
5. Lord you are my cover
6. Lord you are my truth
7. Lord you are my shield
8. Lord you are my defense
9. Lord you are my habitation
10. Lord you are my rock
11. Lord you are the Most High
12. Lord you are my satisfier
13. Lord you are my salvation

Psalm Chapter 92

Prayer Points:
1. I will give thanks unto you oh Lord
2. I will sing praises unto your holy name oh Lord
3. I will show forth your lovingkindness all day long
4. Lord you have made me glad
5. Father exalt my horn like the horn of the unicorn in Jesus name
6. Father anoint me with fresh oil daily in Jesus name
7. May my eyes see my desire on my enemies in Jesus name
8. May my ears hear my desire on the wicked that rise up against me in Jesus name
9. May I flourish like the palm tree in Jesus name
10. May I forever be planted in the house of the Lord in Jesus name
11. May I serve you, praise you, worship you in my old age in Jesus name
12. May I be fruitful in all I do even in my old age in Jesus name

Psalm Chapter 93

Prayer Points:
1. Lord you reign over all the earth
2. Lord you are majestic
3. Lord you are full of strength
4. Lord you are the mighty God
5. Lord you are holy

Psalm Chapter 94

Prayer Points:
1. Father vengance belongs unto you
2. Father defend the widow and the fatherless in Jesus name

3. Father deliver your children from the hand of the wicked in Jesus name
4. Oh Lord teach us your law in Jesus name
5. Father do not cast us off from your presence in Jesus name
6. Father you are our help
7. Lord your mercy upholds us daily
8. Lord you are our defence
9. Lord you are the rock of our refuge

Psalm Chapter 95

Prayer Points:
1. I will make a joyful noise unto the rock of my salvation
2. Father I come before you today with thanksgiving in my heart
3. Father you are the great God
4. Father the hills and everything upon the face of the earth you have made and have authority over
5. Father you are my God and I am yours
6. In Jesus name I will enter into your rest oh Lord

Psalm Chapter 96

Prayer Points:
1. Lord I will sing unto you a new song because you are worthy
2. Father you are a great God and deserve our praise
3. Father you are the maker of the heavens and the earth
4. Father I honor you
5. Father I magnify your holy name
6. Father I worship you
7. Father you reign Lord
8. You are the righteous judge
9. I will rejoice and be glad in you oh Lord

Psalm Chapter 97

Psalm 97: 10 – Ye that love the Lord, hate evil: he preserveth the souls of his saints; he delivereth them out of the hand of the wicked. (KJV)

Prayer points:
1. Lord preserve my soul in Jesus name
2. Lord preserve the soul of my family members in Jesus name
3. Father deliver my soul out of the hand of the wicked in Jesus name
4. Father deliver the souls of my children out of the hand of the wicked in Jesus name
5. Lord deliver the soul of my husband/wife out of the hand of the wicked in Jesus name.
6. Lord deliver the souls of my parents out of the hand of the wicked in Jesus name
7. Lord deliver the souls of my siblings out of the hand of the wicked in Jesus name
8. God I will give you thanks always at the remembrance of your holiness in Jesus name
9. Let my enemies melt away like the hills because of the presence of the Lord in my life in Jesus name. Amen

Psalm Chapter 98

Prayer Points:
1. I will sing unto you Lord God with a new song
2. Father you are a marvelous God
3. Father you are holy
4. Father you are righteous
5. Father you are merciful
6. Father there is no lie in you, you are true and the truth
7. I will make a joyful noise unto you my Lord
8. Let all that is within me praise your holy name

9. Let everything that you have created praise you for you are worthy
10. Father you are the judge of all the earth
11. You are the righteous judge

Psalm Chapter 99

Prayer Points:
1. Lord you are holy
2. I will exalt you oh Lord
3. You are the judge that judges with equity
4. You are the great and mighty God
5. You are great in counsel
6. You are mighty in deed
7. Blessed be your holy name

Psalm Chapter 100

Prayer Points:
1. I will make a joyful noise unto you o Lord
2. I will shout of your greatness with a loud voice
3. I will serve you with gladness
4. I will enter into your gates with thanksgiving and into your court with praise
5. Father you are my Maker
6. I belong to you oh Lord
7. You are a merciful God whose mercy endures forever

Psalm Chapter 101

Prayer Points:
1. Holy Spirit help me to sing of God's mercy and judgement in Jesus name
2. Help me Holy Spirit to behave wisely in Jesus name
3. Help me to walk with a perfect heart in Jesus name

4. Help me Holy Spirit that I will not set any wicked thing before my eyes in Jesus name
5. Spirit of slander I come against you in Jesus name
6. Spirit of pride I come against you in Jesus name

Psalm Chapter 102

Prayer Points:
1. Father deliver me from my enemies in Jesus name
2. Father do not permit my enemies to reproach me in Jesus name
3. May I not eat ashes like bread in Jesus name
4. May I not mingle my drink with tears in Jesus name
5. Father, the time to favor me has come. Favor me oh Lord in Jesus name
6. Father deliver me from premature death in Jesus name
7. Father establish me before you oh Lord in Jesus name

Psalm Chapter 103

Prayer Points:
1. Father everyday will I remember your benefits and glorify your name in Jesus name
2. Father you are the one that forgives my sins and you heal me in times of sickness, I bless you Lord
3. You are the one that saved me from death and showed me your kindness and mercy. Thank you my Father

Psalm Chapter 104

Prayer Points:
1. Father there is none like you in all the earth
2. You are the great and mighty God
3. You are great in counsel
4. You are mighty in deed

5. Father I rejoice in you
6. My thought of you oh Lord shall be sweet in Jesus name
7. I praise you oh Lord for you are worthy in Jesus name

Psalm Chapter 105

Prayer Points:
1. Lord increase me greatly in Jesus name
2. Lord make me stronger than my enemies in Jesus name

Psalm Chapter 106

Prayer Points:
1. Father despite my sins, save me, save my husband, save my children for your name's sake that you might make your mighty power to be known in Jesus name
2. Father save me and my household from the hand of they that hated us in Jesus name
3. Redeem us oh Lord from the hands of our enemies in Jesus name
4. Father let your waters cover our enemies in Jesus name
5. Father let none of our enemies be left in Jesus name
6. Father let the earth open and swallow your enemies in Jesus name
7. Let your fire be kindled in the camp of my enemies, let the flame burn my enemies in Jesus name
8. Father may I not speak unadvisedly with my lips in Jesus name
9. Father may it not go ill with my family and I in Jesus name
10. Father regard my afflictions when I cry unto you in Jesus name
11. Father hear my cry and deliver me out of my distress in Jesus name

Psalm Chapter 107

Prayer Points:
1. Father send your word and heal my marriage in Jesus name
2. Father send your word and heal my home in Jesus name
3. Father send your word and heal my household in Jesus name
4. Father deliver my household and I from all our destructions in Jesus name
5. Father lead my family and I forth to the right way in Jesus name
6. Father satisfy my longing soul in Jesus name
7. Father fill my hungry soul with goodness in Jesus name
8. Father break my bands in sunder in Jesus name
9. Father break the gates of brass and cut the bars of iron in sunder for me in Jesus name
10. Father make the storm in my life a calm in Jesus name
11. Father make still the troubled water in my home in Jesus name

Psalm Chapter 108

Prayer Points:
1. Father help me in my trouble for vain is the help of man in Jesus name
2. Father in heaven, tread down on my enemies in Jesus name
3. Cause me to triumph over my enemies in Jesus name

Psalm Chapter 109

Prayer Points:
1. Your word says that the prayer of the wicked is an abomination to God, father let that be the portion of my persecutors in Jesus name
2. Father as my enemies love cursing, so let it come unto them in Jesus name

3. As my enemies have no delight in blessing, so let blessing be far from them in Jesus name
4. May I not become a reproach in the sight of my enemies in Jesus name
5. Father turn the curse of my enemies to blessing in Jesus name
6. Father let my enemies be put to shame in Jesus name
7. Let confusion be the portion of my enemies in Jesus name

Psalm Chapter 110

Prayer Points:
1. Lord make my enemies my foot stool in Jesus name

Psalm Chapter 111

Prayer Points:
1. Father you are gracious and full of compassion
2. Father give me good understanding in Jesus name

Psalm Chapter 112

Prayer Points:
1. Father may I delight in your commandments in Jesus name
2. Father bless my generation in Jesus name
3. Let light arise in my household even in the midst of darkness in Jesus name
4. Cause my heart to be fixed trusting in you oh Lord in Jesus name
5. Cause me to see my desire on my enemies in Jesus name
6. Father let the desire of the wicked perish in Jesus name

Psalm Chapter 113

Prayer Points:
1. Father, raise the poor out of the dust in Jesus name
2. Father lift up the needy out of the dunghill in Jesus name

3.   Father open the womb of the barren woman that she may bear children in Jesus name
4.   Father destroy every barrenness in me in Jesus name

Psalm Chapter 114

Prayer Points:
1.   Father you are the mighty God
2.   You are the powerful God
3.   You are the miracle working God

Psalm Chapter 115

Prayer Points:
1.   Father I will trust in you for you are my help and my shield
2.   Father increase me and my children more and more in Jesus name

Psalm Chapter 116

Prayer Points:
1.   Lord I will call upon you as long as I live in Jesus name
2.   You are a merciful God
3.   Lord deal bountifully with my soul in Jesus name
4.   Father deliver my household and I from death in Jesus name
5.   Father deliver our eyes from tears in Jesus name

Psalm Chapter 117

Prayer Points:
1.   Father your mercy and your kindness toward my household and I is great
2.   I prasie you Lord for you deserve all the praise

Psalm Chapter 118

Prayer Points:
1. Father you are a good God and your mercy endures forever
2. Father because you are on my side I will not fear in Jesus name
3. Father let me see my desires on them that hate me in Jesus name
4. Father cause my persecutors to be quenched like the fire of the thorns in Jesus name
5. I shall not die, I shall live and I shall declare the works of the Lord in the land of the living in Jesus name
6. The voice of rejoicing and salvation shall be in my home in Jesus name
7. Father this is the day that you have made, I will rejoice and be glad in it in Jesus name
8. Prosper me oh Lord in Jesus name

Psalm Chapter 119

Prayer Points:
1. Father I will hide your word in my heart so that I will not sin against you in Jesus name
2. Father I will meditate on your word, so that I will not go the wrong way in Jesus name
3. Open my eyes oh Lord that I may see the wonders in your word in Jesus name
4. Father may your truth not depart from my mouth in Jesus name
5. Every pit that the proud dug for me, cause them to fall in their pit in Jesus name
6. Father cause me to have more understanding than my teachers in Jesus name
7. Father may your word continually be a lamp unto my feet, and a light unto my path in Jesus name
8. Father you are my hiding place

9. Father you are my shield
10. Father you are my hope
11. Father do not permit the proud to oppress me in Jesus name

Psalm Chapter 120

Prayer Points:
1. Father deliver me from liars in Jesus name
2. Father deliver me from deceitful people in Jesus name
3. Deliver me Lord from them that hate peace in Jesus name
4. Father cause me to seek for peace not war in Jesus name

Psalm Chapter 121

Prayer Points:
1. Father my help comes from you
2. You are the God that does not slumber or sleep
3. Lord you are my keeper in Jesus name
4. Lord you are my shade in Jesus name
5. The sun will not smite me by day in Jesus name
6. The moon will not smite me by night in Jesus name

Psalm Chapter 122

Prayer Points:
1. May my household be glad when we hear – let us go God's house in Jesus name
2. I pray that there will be peace in Jerusalem in Jesus name
3. I pray that there will be peace within my walls in Jesus name
4. Father let there be prosperity within my home in Jesus name

Psalm Chapter 123

Prayer Points:
1. Father you are a merciful God
2. Have mercy on me oh God in Jesus name

Psalm Chapter 124

Prayer Points:
1. Father thank you for delivering my family and I from the hand of the enemy in Jesus name
2. Thank you Father for delivering us from the overwhelming waters in Jesus name
3. Thank you Father for delivering us from pride in Jesus name
4. Thank you Father for providing way of escape for us out of the snare of our enemies in Jesus name
5. Father our help is in you the maker of heaven and earth

Psalm Chapter 125

Prayer Points:
1. Father cause your presence to be around my family and I in Jesus name
2. Do not allow the rod of the wicked to rest on us in Jesus name
3. Father let peace be upon my household and I in Jesus name

Psalm Chapter 126

Prayer Points:
1. Father turn again my captivity in Jesus name
2. Father fill my mouth with laughter in Jesus name
3. Father fill my tongue with singing in Jesus name
4. Father do great things for me in Jesus name

Psalm Chapter 127

Prayer Points:
1. Father may I not labor in vain in Jesus name
2. May I not eat the bread of sorrow in Jesus name
3. Father give me and my household sleep in Jesus name

Psalm Chapter 128

Prayer Points:
1. May the fear of the Lord be in me in Jesus name
2. May I eat the labor of my hands in Jesus name
3. May I be happy all the days of my life in Jesus name
4. May it be well with me oh Lord in Jesus name
5. May I see my children's children in Jesus name

Psalm Chapter 129

Prayer Points:
1. Father thank you for not allowing the enemy to prevail against me in Jesus name
2. Father I thank you for cutting asunder the cords of the wicked in Jesus name
3. Father cause my enemies to be like the grass that grows on a barren land, which withers before it grows up in Jesus name

Psalm Chapter 130

Prayer Points:
1. Father when I cry unto you, hear me in Jesus name
2. Father forgive all my transgressions in Jesus name
3. Father I will hope in you continually in Jesus name

Psalm Chapter 131

Prayer Points:
1. I come against the spirit of pride in Jesus name
2. I receive the spirit of humility in Jesus name
3. My hope is in you oh Lord my God

Psalm Chapter 132

Prayer Points:
1. Father I open up my heart for you to dwell in in Jesus name
2. Father make my horn bud in Jesus name
3. Father clothe my enemies with shame in Jesus name
4. Cause me to flourish in this land oh Lord my God

Psalm Chapter 133

Prayer Points:
1. I pray for the spirit of peace among brethren in Jesus name
2. I pray for the spirit of unity among brethren in Jesus name
3. I pray for the spirit of love among brethren in Jesus name

Psalm Chapter 134

Prayer Points:
1. Father I praise you the Maker of heaven and earth
2. Blessed be your holy name in Jesus name

Psalm Chapter 135

Prayer Points:
1. Father I praise you for you are good
2. Thank you Father for choosing me as your child
3. Father you are a great God that is above all gods
4. Father even nature itself is subject to your command

Psalm Chapter 136

Prayer Points:
1. Father I give you thanks for you are a good God and your mercy endures forever
2. Father you are the Maker of the heaven and the earth

Psalm Chapter 137

Prayer Points:
1. Father deliver us from the hands of our captors in Jesus name

Psalm Chapter 138

Prayer Points:
1. Father, in the name of Jesus I praise you with my whole heart
2. Thank you Father for answering me when I cry unto you in Jesus name
3. Thank you Father for strengthening my soul in Jesus name
4. Thank you Father for reviving me even in the midst of trouble in Jesus name
5. Father stretch out your hand and save me from the wrath of my enemies in Jesus name
6. Father perfect everything that concerns me for your glory in Jesus name
7. Father do not forsake me in Jesus name

Psalm Chapter 139

Prayer Points:
1. Father you are the God that knows the thought of my heart
2. Father you are my provider and my protector
3. You are the almighty God whom nothing is hid from
4. Thank you Father for making me fearfully and wonderfully in Jesus name
5. Thank you because I am precious in your eyes in Jesus name
6. Father your enemies are my enemies and my enemies are your enemies
7. Father search my heart and cleanse me from any wickedness in Jesus name

Psalm Chapter 140

Prayer Points:
1. Father deliver and preserve my household and I from our enemies in Jesus name
2. Father cause the enemy to be caught in the net they spread for me in Jesus name
3. Father cover my head in the day of battle in Jesus name
4. Father put an end to the devices of the wicked in Jesus name
5. Let the mischief of my enemies lips backfire in Jesus name

Psalm Chapter 141

Prayer Points:
1. Father do not delay to help me when I cry unto you in Jesus name
2. Father may my prayers ascend unto you as an incense in Jesus name
3. Holy Spirit take control of the words that proceed out of my mouth that I may not sin in words in Jesus name
4. Set a watch over my heart and mind that I will not think of any evil in Jesus name
5. Father my trust is in you only in Jesus name
6. Cause me to escape from the net and pit of the enemy, while the enemy is caught in them in Jesus name

Psalm Chapter 142

Prayer Points:
1. I will not be caught by the snares the enemy has laid for me in Jesus name
2. Father my trust is not in any man, for man will fail me
3. Father you are my refuge
4. Father you are my portion forever in Jesus name

5. Father deliver me from the enemies that are stronger than I am in Jesus name
6. Set me free from the my enemy's prison in Jesus name

Psalm Chapter 143

Prayer Points:
1. Deliver my spirit from being overwhelmed in Jesus name
2. Deliver my heart from desolation in Jesus name
3. Cause me to meditate daily on your works in Jesus name
4. Cause my soul to thirst for you as a thirsty land in Jesus name
5. Holy Spirit direct my steps in the way that I should go in Jesus name
6. Father you are my hiding place from my enemies in Jesus name
7. Destroy every power that afflicts my soul for your name's sake in Jesus name

Psalm Chapter 144

Prayer Points:
1. Father you are the only one that can teach my hands to war and my fingers to fight, therefore teach my hands and fingers to war and fight in Jesus name
2. Father you are my goodness
3. Father you are my fortress
4. Father you are my high tower
5. Father you are my shield
6. Father my trust is in you
7. Father deliver me from the hand of the wicked in Jesus name
8. Father prosper me oh Lord in Jesus name
9. Father enlarge my coast oh Lord in Jesus name

Psalm Chapter 145

Prayer Points:
1. Father, there is none like you in all the earth
2. You are an awesome God
3. Father cause me to call upon you in truth in Jesus name
4. Father fulfill my hearts desire in Jesus name
5. Father save me in Jesus name

Psalm Chapter 146

Prayer Points:
1. Father you are the righteous God
2. Father judge my oppressors in Jesus name
3. Father set me free from every form of bondage in Jesus name
4. Father open my spiritual eyes in Jesus name
5. Father turn the way of the wicked upside down in Jesus name

Psalm Chapter 147

Prayer Points:
1. Father heal my broken heart in Jesus name
2. Father give me this day my daily bread in Jesus name
3. Father bless my children in Jesus name
4. Surround me oh God with peace in Jesus name

Psalm Chapter 148

Prayer Points:
1. Father you are the Creator of heaven and earth
2. Father you alone are the excellent God

Psalm Chapter 149

Prayer Points:
1. Holy Spirit put a new song in my mouth to the Almighty Father in Jesus name
2. Holy Spirit cause me to rejoice in my Maker the Almighty Father in Jesus name
3. When I am upon my bed, Holy Spirit cause me to sing aloud unto my Father in Jesus name
4. I receive every honor that belongs to the saints in Jesus name

Psalm Chapter 150

Prayer Points:
1. Father because I have breath, I will praise you in Jesus name
2. Father I will praise you with dancing in Jesus name
3. Father I will praise you with any kind of instruments that I have available to me in Jesus name
4. Father I will praise you with clapping in Jesus name
5. Praise the Lord. Halleluah.

Prayer Points from Ecclesiastes

Chapter 1

Ecclesiates Chapter 1:18

Prayer Points:
1. May the wisdom that I have not bring me grief in Jesus name
2. May the wisdom that I have cause me to have the fear of the Lord in Jesus name
3. May the knowledge that I have not bring me sorrow in Jesus name
4. May the increased knowledge that I am daily seeking not bring me increased sorrow in Jesus name.

Chapter 2

Ecclesiates Chapter 2:26

Prayer Points:
1. Father may my life be good in your sight in Jesus name
2. Father, give me wisdom as good man in your sight in Jesus name
3. Father, give me knowledge in Jesus name
4. Father, give me joy in Jesus name
5. Father, I refuse to travail in vain in Jesus name

Chapter 3

Ecclesiates 3:13

Prayer Points:
1. Father grant that I will eat and drink, and enjoy the good of my labor in Jesus name
2. I will not labor in vain in Jesus name
3. Father I receive your gift with open hands to eat and drink and enjoy the good of my labor in Jesus name

Chapter 4

Ecclesiates 4:9-10

Prayer Points:
1. May I never be alone in Jesus name
2. May I never lack helper in Jesus name

Chapter 5

Ecclesiates 5:1-4

Prayer Points:
1. Let the spirit of holiness come upon me in Jesus name

2. Let the spirit of righteousness come upon me in Jesus name
3. Father may I be a hearer and a doer of your word in Jesus name
4. May I be quick to hear in the name of Jesus
5. I receive spirit of obedience in Jesus name
6. May I be slow to speak in Jesus name
7. Holy Spirit, help me not to be hasty to utter anything before God in Jesus name
8. Holy Spirit, guard my mouth in Jesus name
9. Holy Spirit have perfect control of my mouth in Jesus name
10. Holy Spirit, help me with my prayer and intersession so that I will pray in accordance to the will of God for my life because you know the will of God
11. Help me Holy Spirit to pay my vow to the Lord in Jesus name
12. Help me Holy Spirit not to defer any of my vows to the Lord in Jesus name
13. Father forgive me for the vows that I made in the past and failed to pay them especially those that I have forgotten about in Jesus name
14. Father, I repent of every vow that I made in the past and failed to pay.
15. Holy Spirit, bring to my remembrance those vows that I have forgotten so that I can pay them in Jesus name

Chapter 7

Ecclesiates 7:1-14

Prayer Points:
1. I will seek good name instead of precious ointment in Jesus name
2. May the gift of God upon me not destroy me in Jesus name
3. May the gift of God upon me not destroy another in Jesus name
4. May the gift of God upon my life build me in Jesus name

5. May the gift of God upon my life build my neighbor in Jesus name
6. May the gift of God upon my life bring glory to the name of the Almighty Father in Jesus name
7. I reject the spirit of pride in Jesus name.
8. I receive the spirit of humility in Jesus name
9. I confess that I will not be hasty in my spirit to be angry in Jesus name
10. May the wisdom that I have give life and not bring death in Jesus name
11. I receive the grace to rejoice in whatever situation comes my way in Jesus name

Chapter 10

Ecclesiates 10:8

Prayer Points:
1. I will not fall into any undeserved pit in Jesus name
2. I will not dig any pit for my brethren to fall in, in Jesus name
3. Any one that digs a pit for me will fall into the pit in Jesus name
4. Any one that digs a pit for any member of my household will fall into the pit in Jesus name
5. I will not break the hedge with lying for the serpent to bite me in Jesus name
6. I will not break the hedge with hate for the serpent to bite me in Jesus name
7. I will not break the hedge with envy for the serpent to bite me in Jesus name
8. I will not break the hedge with pride for the serpent to bite me in Jesus name
9. I will not break the hedge with any form of sin for the serpent to bite me in Jesus name
10. Help me Holy Spirit

Chapter 11

Ecclesiates 11: 1-10

Prayer Points:
1. I receive the spirit of giving in Jesus name
2. Even as I give, may I give joyfully in Jesus name
3. Even as I give, may it be given unto me good measure shaken together and running over in Jesus name.
4. Even as I give, may all my work be blessed in Jesus name
5. Even as I give may all that I put my hands in prosper in Jesus name
6. I receive grace to trust God at all times in Jesus name
7. I receive the grace to praise God at all times, in season and out of season in Jesus name
8. Holy Spirit remove every sorrow from my heart in Jesus name
9. Holy Spirit put away evil from my flesh in Jesus name
10. Cleanse me from every form of filthiness of the flesh in Jesus name
11. Cleanse me from every form of filthiness of the spirit in Jesus name
12. Holy Spirit, perfect holiness in me in Jesus name

Chapter 12

Ecclesisates 12:13-14

Prayer Points:
1. I will fear God in Jesus name
2. I will keep God's commandments in Jesus name
3. I will perform all the duties required of me as a child of God in the name of Jesus
4. When I am judged, may no evil be found in me in Jesus name

Isaiah Chapter 6

Isaiah 6: 1-13

Prayer Points:
1. Everything that represents king Uzziah in my life – I command you to die in Jesus name
2. Everything that represents king Uzziah in the life of my children I command you to die in Jesus name
3. May I see the glory of the Lord upon me and my children in Jesus name
4. May I see the favor of God in my life in Jesus name
5. May I see the favor of God in the lives of members of my household in Jesus name
6. May I experience the blessing of God upon my life in Jesus name
7. May members of my household experience the blessing of the Lord in Jesus name
8. Father touch my mouth and take away my iniquity in Jesus name
9. Purge me of my sins in Jesus name
10. Father may I always be ready spirit, soul and body to do your will in Jesus name
11. May I hear your voice when you speak in Jesus name

Isaiah Chapter 7

Isaiah 7: 1-25

Prayer Points:
1. Every evil counsel of the enemy shall not stand in Jesus name
2. Every evil counsel of the enemy shall not come to pass in the name of Jesus
3. Lord reveal unto me every evil counsel of the enemy in Jesus name

4. Lord, let every evil counsel of the enemy backfire in the name of Jesus

5. Every evil counsel of the enemy assigned against me shall not see the light of day in Jesus name

6. Every evil counsel of the enemy assigned against me shall pass away as the untimely birth of a woman in Jesus name

7. Father, break down every power that plans evil counsel against me in Jesus name

8. May I not tempt the Lord in Jesus name

Isaiah Chapter 19

Isaiah 19: 2 – 4. And I will set the Egyptians against the Egyptians: and they shall fight every one against his brother; and every one against his neighbour; city against city, and kingdom against kingdom. 3 – And the spirit of Egypt shall fall in the midst thereof; and I will destroy the counsel thereof: and they shall seek to the idols, and to the charmer, and to them that have familiar spirits, and to the wizards. 4 – And the Egyptians will I give over into the hand of a cruel lord; and a fierce king shall rule over them, saith the Lord, the Lord of hosts. (KJV)

Prayer points:
1. Father, set my enemies against my enemies in Jesus name

2. Let my enemies fight everyone against his brother, sister, father, mother, relatives, friends, neighbours in Jesus name

3. Father destroy the spirit of my enemies in Jesus name

4. Father destroy the counsel of my enemies in Jesus name

5. Father give my enemies over to the cruel Lords in Jesus name

6. Father, let a fierce king rule over my enemies in Jesus name.

Isaiah Chapter 22

Prayer points:
1. Father, every door that you have opened for me, may no man be able to shut in Jesus name
2. Father, every evil door that you have shut on my behalf, may no man be able to open it in Jesus name
3. Father, fasten me as a nail to you in Jesus name. Amen

Isaiah Chapter 26

Isaiah 26: 17. Like as a woman with child, that draweth near the time of her delivery, is in pain, and crieth out in her pangs; so have we been in thy sight, O Lord. (KJV)

Prayer points:
1. Father, in the name of Jesus I cry to you this day like a woman with child that draweth near the time of her delivery, is in pain, and crieth out in her pangs, so have I been in your sight, lord. Deliver me Lord from the hands of my oppressors in Jesus name
2. Deliver my husband/wife from the hands of the oppressors in Jesus name
3. Deliver my children from the hands of the oppressors in Jesus name
4. Deliver my parents from the hands of the oppressors in Jesus name.

Isaiah Chapter 27

Isaiah 27: 2-3. In that day sing ye unto her, A vineyard of red wine. 3- I the Lord do keep it; I will water it every moment: lest any hurt it, I will keep it night and day. (KJV)

Prayer points:

1. Lord keep me like the vineyards of red wine in Jesus name
2. Lord, water me every moment in Jesus name
3. Let no hurt come upon me in Jesus name
4. Father, keep me night and day in Jesus name.

Isaiah Chapter 31

Isaiah 31: 1-2 - Woe to them that go down to Egypt for help; and stay on horses, and trust in chariots, because they are many; and in horsemen, because they are strong; but they look not unto the Holy One of Israel, neither seek the Lord. 2 – Yet he also is wise, and will bring evil, and will not call back his word: but will arise against the house of the evildoers, and against the help of them that work iniquity. (KJV)

Prayer points:

1. Father, arise against the house of the evildoers.
2. Bring evil upon my enemies
3. Bring evil against the help of my enemies
4. Bring evil against they that work iniquities in Jesus name.

Isaiah Chapter 37

Isaiah 37: 6b, 7, - Be not afraid of the words that thou hast heard, wherewith the servants of the kings of Assyria have blasphemed me. 7 – Behold, I will send a blast upon him, and he shall hear a rumour, and return to his own land; and I will cause him to fall by the sword in his own land. (KJV)

Prayer points:

1. In the name of Jesus, I will not be afraid of the report of my enemies.
2. I will not be afraid of the blasphemy of my enemies against my God

3. Father, send a blast upon my enemies in Jesus name
4. Father, send a blast upon my tormentors in Jesus name
5. Father, send a blast upon my oppressors in Jesus name
6. Father, send a blast upon they that seek my life in Jesus name
7. Let my enemies hear a rumour and return to their abode and leave me alone in Jesus name.
8. Father cause my enemies to fall by the sword in their land in Jesus name

Hezekiah's prayer to the Lord

Vs 16 –20.

1. *O Lord of hosts, God of Israel, that dwells between the cherubims, thou art the God, even thou alone, of all the kingdoms of the earth*
2. *Thou God hast made the heavens and earth.*
3. *Incline your ear, O Lord, and hear;*
4. *Open your eyes, O Lord, and see*
5. *Hear Lord, all the words of my enemies, which have sent to reproach the living God.*
6. *O Lord our God, save us*
7. *Save us from the hands of our enemies that all the earth may know that thou art the Lord, even you only.*
8. Lord you are the God that knows my thoughts
9. Lord you are the God that knows my deeds
10. Lord you are the God that knows my secrets.
11. God, you know my going out and my coming in.
12. Have mercy on me Lord
13. May I not sin against you in words, thoughts and deeds in Jesus name.
14. Father, defend me
15. Father, save me for your name sake and for your son's sake in Jesus name

Isaiah Chapter 38

Isaiah Chapter 38:1-22

Prayer Points:
1. Father defend my life in Jesus name
2. Father defend my health in Jesus name
3. Father defend my household in Jesus name
4. Father defend my buisness in Jesus name
5. Father defend my career in Jesus name
6. Father defend my spiritual life in Jesus name
7. Father defend my finances in Jesus name
8. Father defend all that concerns me in Jesus name

Isaiah Chapter 60

Prayer points:
1. I will arise and I will shine, for my light has come and the glory of the Lord has risen on me
2. The glory of the Lord shall be upon me
3. People shall come to my light, and kings to the brightness of my rising
4. Everyone that despised me shall bow themselves down at the soles of my feet and I shall be called the city of the Lord
5. God will make excellent all that concern me, and He will make me a joy of many generations
6. I acknowledge the Lord is my Savior and my Redeemer, the mighty one of Jacob
7. Violence shall no more be heard in my home
8. Violence shall no more be heard in my life
9. Violence shall no more be heard in my family
10. Violence shall no more be heard in my marriage
11. There shall be no wasting within my borders
12. There shall be no destruction within my borders
13. The Lord shall be unto me an everlasting light

14. God shall be my glory
15. My sun shall not go down
16. My moon shall not withdraw itself
17. The Lord shall be my everlasting light
18. The days of my mourning are ended
19. All my household shall be righteous
20. All my household shall inherit this land forever
21. The Lord will hasten these confessions of mine in Jesus name

Isaiah Chapter 62

Prayer points:
1. For my sake, O God hold not your peace
2. For my family's sake O God do not rest unitl our enemies are defeated in Jesus name.
3. My family and I shall be called by a new name in Jesus name
4. My family and I shall be a crown of glory in the hand of the Lord
5. My family and I shall be a royal diadem in the hand of my God
6. My family and I shall no more be termed 'forsaken' neither shall our home any more be termed 'desolate'
7. I shall be called 'Hephzibah'
8. My family shall be called Beulah, for the Lord has delighted in us
9. The Lord shall rejoice over my family and I in Jesus name
10. The Lord shall not give my corn to be meat for my enemies
11. The sons of the stranger will not drink my wine for which I have labored in Jesus name

Isaiah Chapter 65

Prayer points:
1. I shall not build and another inhabits
2. I shall not plant and another eats
3. I shall build and inhabit

4. I shall plant and eat
5. I shall enjoy the works of my hands
6. I shall not labor in vain in Jesus name
7. I shall not bring forth trouble in Jesus name
8. My offsprings and I are the seed of the blessed of the Lord
9. Before I call, my God will answer
10. While I am yet speaking, my God will hear in Jesus name

Jeremiah Chapter 1

1. Thank you Lord for knowing me before you formed me in my mother's womb.
2. Thank you Lord for sanctifying me before I came out of the womb
3. Thank you Lord for ordaining me as a prophet unto the nations
4. Lord I will obey your word, I will not be afraid of the faces of the enemy in Jesus name
5. Thank you Lord for your promise to be with me, to deliver me in Jesus name
6. Thank you Lord for putting your words in my mouth in Jesus name
7. Thank you Lord for setting me over the kingdoms, to root out, and to pull down, and to destroy, and to throw down, to build, and to plant in Jesus name.
8. Father, hasten your word to perform it in my home in Jesus name
9. Father, hasten your word to perform it in my marriage in Jesus name
10. Father, hasten your word to perform it in the life of my children in Jesus name
11. Father hasten your word to perform it in my spiritual life in Jesus name
12. Father hasten your word to perform it in the life of as many as I am lifting up to you for the salvation of their souls.
13. Father, I thank you for making me a defense city.

14. Thank you Father for making me an iron pillar
15. Thank you Father for making me brasen walls against the whole land
16. Thank you Father that my enemies shall not prevail in Jesus name

Jeremiah Chapter 3

Jeremiah chapter 3: 15

Prayer Points:
1. Father give your people pastors according to your own heart in Jesus name
2. Father give your people pastors that will feed them with knowledge in Jesus name
3. Father give your people pastors that will feed them with understanding in Jesus name

Jeremiah Chapter 5

Jeremiah chapter 5:14

Prayer Points:
1. Father make your words in my mouth fire in Jesus name
2. Father make my enemies wood in the name of Jesus name
3. Father cause your word in my mouth which is fire to devour my enemies which you have made wood in Jesus name.

Jeremiah Chapter 6

Jeremiah chapter 6: 16

Prayer Points:
1. Almghty Father, where is the old path?
2. Father where is the good way?
3. Father let your spirit lead me in the good way in Jesus name

4. Father, let my soul find rest in the path that you will lead me in Jesus name

Jeremiah Chapter 9

Jeremiah chapter 9:23-24

Prayer Points:
1. I will not glory in my wisdom in Jesus name
2. I will not glory in my might in Jesus name
3. I will not glory in my riches in Jesus name
4. I will glory in my understanding of the Lord in Jesus name
5. I will glory that I know the Almighty Father in Jesus name
6. I will glory in the God that exercises loving kindness in Jesus name
7. I will glory in the God that is righteous in Jesus name
8. I will glory in the God that exercises judgment in Jesus name
9. I will delight in the Lord Maker of heaven and earth

Jeremiah Chapter 15

Jeremiah Chapter 15:1-20

Prayer Points:
1. Father appoint four kinds of destruction over the powers that war against me in Jesus name
2. Father appoint the sword to slay the powers that are warring against me in Jesus name
3. Father appoint the dogs to tear the powers that are warring against me in Jesus name
4. Father appoint the fowls of the heaven to devour the powers that are warring against me in Jesus name
5. Father appoint the beasts of the earth to destroy the powers that are warring against me in Jesus name

6. Make me a fenced brasen wall against my enemies in Jesus name
7. When my enemies fight against me, cause them not to prevail against me in Jesus name
8. Father be with me at all times in Jesus name
9. Father save me from my enemies in Jesus name
10. Father deliver me from my enemies in Jesus name

Jeremiah Chapter 17

1. Father, I want my trust to be in you, and I want you to be my hope that I may be blessed
2. Father, may I be as a tree planted by the waters, may my roots spread and may I not see when trouble comes because you are my shield, my glory and the lifter up of my head in Jesus name.
3. May I prosper continually in Jesus name.
4. May I not be worried about my enemies or trouble because my family and I are hid under the shadow of your wings Lord.
5. May I not cease to grow spiritually and financially. Even as you have commanded that I should be fruitful and multiply, so shall it be in Jesus name.
6. Father keep my heart clean in Jesus name
7. Father keep my family and I safe from those with deceitful and desperately wicked hearts in Jesus name
8. Father may I not seek wealth by false means in Jesus name
9. Heal me Lord and I shall be healed in Jesus name.
10. Save me Lord and I shall be saved.
11. Father, you are the fountain of living waters.
12. Father, confound they that persecute me in Jesus name
13. Let my enemies be dismayed in Jesus name.
14. Bring upon my enemies the day of evil and destroy them with double destruction in Jesus name.

Jeremiah Chapter 20

Jeremiah Chapter 20: 11

Prayer Points:
1. The Lord is with me as the mighty terrible one in Jesus name
2. My persecutors shall stumble in Jesus name
3. My persecutors shall not prevail in Jesus name
4. My persecutors shall be greatly ashamed in Jesus name
5. My persecutors shall not prosper in Jesus name
6. My persecutors shall be confused in Jesus name

Jeremiah Chapter 24

Jeremiah Chapter 24:6

Prayer Points:
1. Father set your eyes upon me for good in Jesus name
2. Father bring me to your promised land in Jesus name
3. Father build me in Jesus name
4. Father do not pull me down in Jesus name
5. Father plant my feet upon Christ the Solid Rock in Jesus name
6. Father do not pluck me away in Jesus name
7. Father give me a heart to know you in Jesus name
8. Father may I be called your people all the days of my life in Jesus name
9. Father be my God from now, even unto the end in Jesus name
10. May I serve you with my whole heart in Jesus name

Jeremiah Chapter 51

Prayer points:
1. I am God's battle axe and weapon of war
2. My children are God's battle axe and weapon of war
3. God will use me to break in pieces the horse and its rider
4. God will use me to break in pieces man and woman

5. With me God will break in pieces old and young
6. With me God will break in pieces young man and maiden
7. God will use me to break in pieces the shepherd and his flock
8. God will use me to break in pieces the husbandman and his yoke of oxen
9. God will use me to break in pieces the captain and rulers in Jesus name

Lamentations Chapter 2

Lamentations 2: 16 - All thine enemies have opened their mouth against thee: they hiss and gnash the teeth: they say, we have swallowed her up: certainly this is the day that we looked for; we have found, we have seen it. (KJV)

Prayer points:
1. Father, may my enemies not rejoice over me in Jesus name
2. May the joy of my enemies over me be turned to sorrow in Jesus name
3. May the expectations of my enemies not come to pass in the name of Jesus
4. May the triumph of my enemies be turned to defeat over my enemies in Jesus name
5. May my enemies mouth not be able to open against me anymore forever in Jesus name
6. May my enemies not be able to hiss over me in Jesus name
7. May my enemies not be able to gnash their teeth over me in Jesus name
8. May my enemies not be able to swallow me up in Jesus name
9. Every of my property that my enemies have swallowed up may they not have rest until they have vomited every one of them in Jesus name.
10. May my enemies not see the day that they are looking forward to seeing in Jesus name.

11. May my enemies not see and or find what they are looking for in Jesus name.

Ezekiel Chapter 1

Prayer points:
1. Father in my captivity, let me experience open heavens
2. Father in my desert hour, let me experience open heaven
3. Father in my captivity let me see visions of God
4. Father let your word come expressly to me
5. Let your hand be upon me for good
6. Father cause me to see your glory
7. Father cause me to hear your voice when you speak

Ezekiel Chapter 2

Prayer points:
1. Spirit of the living God, come into me
2. Spirit of the living God, take total control of me
3. Spitit of the living God, set me on my feet
4. Father let your Spirit cause me to hear you
5. Father here I am, send me
6. Cause me to speak your words
7. I will not be afraid of the words of man
8. Spirit of disobedience I come against you
9. Spirit of fear, I come against you

Ezekiel Chapter 3

Prayer points:
1. Father to those you are sending me to, make my face strong against their faces
2. Father to those you are sending me to, make my forehead strong against their foreheads
3. Cause me not to be afraid of the rebellious

4. Father, I hear your words with my ears
5. Father, I receive your words in my heart
6. Father make me a watchman unto your people
7. May I not be afraid to speak your word as you command me to speak
8. Father cause me to speak when I need to speak
9. Father cause me to be quiet when I need to be quiet

Ezekiel Chapter 12

Prayer points:
1. None of God's promises to me will be prolonged any more
2. Every word that God has spoken to me shall come to pass
3. Every promise of God for my life shall no longer be prolonged, it shall come to pass
4. Every promise of God for my family shall no longer be prolonged, it shall come to pass in Jesus name

Ezekiel Chapter 13: 22

Prayer points:
1. Because the wicked have made my heart sad with their lies and strengthened their own hands and continue in their wickedness, God will deliver me out of their hand in Jesus name. Amen.
2. God will fight for me
3. The enemy will not rejoice over me in Jesus name

Ezekiel Chapter 30

Ezekiel 30: 24 - And I will strengthen the arms of the king of Babylon, and put sword in his hand: but I will break Pharaoh's arms, and he shall groan before him with the groaning of deadly wounded man. (KJV)

Prayer points:
1. Father, strengthen my arms in Jesus name
2. Father, put your sword in my hand
3. Father, break the arms of my enemies
4. Make my enemies groan with groaning of a deadly wounded man in Jesus name.
5. Father, scatter my enemies
6. Father, disperse my enemies that they may know that I serve the living God in Jesus name

Daniel Chapter 2: 47

Prayer points:
1. Father may my life be pleasing unto you in Jesus name
2. Father do something new in my life in Jesus name
3. Father cause believers and unbelievers to say that my God is a God of gods and a Lord of Kings in Jesus name

Daniel

Prayer points:
1. Father, may I be known as a woman/man of God in whom is the spirit of the holy God in Jesus name. 5 vs. 11
2. Father grant that an excellent spirit will be upon me in Jesus name. 6 vs. 3a
3. Father may I be preferred wherever I go and in whatever I do in Jesus name. 6 vs. 3b.
4. Let the fault that the enemies will find in me be that I serve God in spirit and in truth in Jesus name.
5. Father may my ways be pleasing to you that my enemies will seek to deliver me in Jesus name. 6 vs. 14
6. My enemies, because of the power and favor of God upon my life will be forced to pray for me in Jesus name. 6 vs. 16b
7. Anybody that does me harm, will loose sleep in Jesus name
8. Anybody that does me harm will loose appetite in Jesus name

9. Anybody that does me harm will not have peace in Jesus name. 6 vs. 18.

10. Those that plan evil for my family & I, evil will befall them in Jesus name. 6 vs. 24.

11. Father, give me revelation in Jesus name

12. Father give me understanding in Jesus name

13. Father give me vision in Jesus name 10 vs. 1

14. Father give me the grace to chastise myself before you in Jesus name

15. May I set my heart to understand in Jesus name

16. Hear my words O Lord

17. Come for my words O God. 10 vs. 12

18. Father send your angels to fight against the prince of the air that is withholding my miracle in Jesus name

19. Father, send your angels to fight against the prince of the air that is withholding my blessings in Jesus name

20. Father send your angels to fight against the prince of the air that is holding back my breakthrough in Jesus name. 10 vs. 13

21. Prince of Persia, I come against you in Jesus name.

22. Prince of the air, I come against you by the power that is in the blood of Jesus. 10 vs. 13

23. Let the words that weaken me, be the words that will strengthen me again in Jesus name.

24. Father, I want to know you that I may do exploit in accordance to your word, 'but the people that know their God shall be strong, and do exploits'. 11 vs. 32b.

25. Father, may my children know you that they can do exploits in Jesus name

26. Father may my husband/wife know you that he/she can do exploits in Jesus name

27. Father, may my whole family know you that we can do exploits in Jesus name.

28. Father I pray for wisdom, that I may shine as the brightness of the firmament

29. Father, I pray for the grace to turn many to righteousness, that I may be as the stars forever and ever in Jesus name. 12 vs. 3

Hosea

Prayer points

1. Have mercy upon my house O Lord
2. Have mercy upon my husband/wife
3. Have mercy upon me O Lord
4. Have mercy upon my children O Lord
5. Have mercy upon my parents O Lord
6. Have mercy upon my siblings O Lord
7. Save my father in Jesus name
8. Save my children O Lord
9. Save my husband/wife O Lord
10. Save my siblings O Lord
11. Save my parents O Lord 1 vs. 7
12. Father, may I not be destroyed for lack of knowledge in Jesus name
13. May I seek knowledge in Jesus name
14. May I get knowledge in Jesus name
15. May I not reject knowledge in Jesus name.
16. Do not reject me Lord. 4 vs. 6

Joel

Prayer points:
1. I will turn to you Lord with all my heart
2. I will turn to you Lord with weeping
3. I will turn to you Lord with fasting
4. I will turn to you Lord with mourning. 2 vs. 12
5. I will rent my heart Lord and not my garment in Jesus name
6. I will turn unto you my Lord and my God. 2 vs. 13
7. Lord you are a gracious God

8. You are a merciful God
9. You are God that is slow to anger
10. You are full of great kindness. 2 vs. 13
11. I will be glad and rejoice in you Lord for giving me the former rain and the latter rain. 2 vs. 23
12. Father restore to me the years that the locust hath eaten
13. Father restore to me the years that the cankerworm hath eaten
14. Father restore to me the years that the caterpillar hath eaten.
15. Father restore to me Lord the years that the palmerworm hath eaten. 2 vs. 25
16. Father, may I eat in plenty
17. May I be satisfied
18. May I praise the name of the Lord
19. May I never be ashamed
20. Father, you are my God and there is no one else
21. Father, deliver me even as I call upon your name
22. Father, let there be deliverance in mount Zion and Jerusalem.
23. I am strong in Jesus name 3 vs. 10b
24. Let my enemies be desolate for their violence against the children of God 3 vs. 19

Amos

Prayer points:
1. Father, may I seek you daily in Jesus name
2. Father, may I not seek evil in Jesus name 5 vs. 14
3. Father, may I not be at ease in Zion in Jesus name 6 vs. 1

Obadiah

Prayer points:
1. Father, let there be deliverance upon mount Zion in accordance to your word in Jesus name
2. Father, let there be holiness in the body of Christ

3. Father, may the children of God possess their possession in Jesus name. Amen

Jonah

Prayer points:
1. Father may I sacrifice unto you the voice of thanksgiving in Jesus name
2. Father, I pray that I will pay whatever I have vowed in Jesus name 2 vs. 9
3. Father, may I believe every one of your words in Jesus name 3 vs. 5
4. God, thou art a gracious God
5. Lord thou art a merciful God
6. Lord thou art slow to anger and of great kindness 4 vs. 2b

Micah

Prayer points:
1. Father, may I not devise iniquity in Jesus name
2. Father may I not work evil upon my bed in Jesus name
3. Father, may I do that which you require of me in Jesus name
4. Father, may I do justice
5. Father, may I love mercy.
6. Father, may I walk humbly with you in Jesus name 6 vs. 8
7. Father you are my light in darkness 7 vs. 8

Nahum

Prayer points:
1. Father, you are a good God, teach me holy spirit to be good
2. Father, be my stronghold in time of trouble
3. Father, you know them that trust in you, help me Holy Spirit to put all my trust in the Lord in Jesus name. 1 vs. 7

4. In the name of Jesus, affliction shall not arise a second time. Amen. 1 vs. 9b
5. Father, break the yoke of the enemy from off me, bust my bonds asunder in Jesus name. 1 vs. 13.
6. May the wicked not have dominion over me in Jesus name

Habakkuk

Prayer points:
1. Father, I pray for the grace to wait for the vision. Your word says that it will surely come, it will not tarry. Father I believe and I receive in Jesus name. 2 vs. 3
2. Father let the earth be filled with the knowledge of the glory of the Lord, as the waters cover the sea 2 vs. 14
3. I will rejoice in the Lord, in the God of my salvation will I have joy
4. Lord God, be my strength
5. Lord make my feet like hinds' feet
6. Father make me to walk upon mine high places. 3 vs. 19

Zephaniah

Prayer points:
1. Father, may the gods of my enemies become a booty
2. May the houses of my enemies become desolate.
3. May my enemies build houses and not inhabit the house
4. May my enemies not drink of the wine from the vineyards they planted 1 vs. 13
5. I will not do iniquity
6. I will not speak lies
7. My tongue will not speak deceit
8. I shall feed and lie down
9. None shall make me ashamed in Jesus name 3 vs. 13
10. Father, make me a name and a praise among all people of the earth

11. Father, turn back my captivity before my eyes, set me free 3 vs. 20

Haggai

Prayer points:
1. Father shake the heavens and the earth, and the sea and the dry land
2. Father shake all nations
3. Father fill me with glory

Zechariah

Prayer points:
1. Father, be unto my family and I as a wall of fire round about us in Jesus name
2. Father, be the glory in the midst of my family in Jesus name
3. Thank you Father for calling me the apple of your eye. 3 vs.5 & 8b
4. Who art thou, O great mountain before me, thou shall become a plain in Jesus name. 4 vs. 7
5. Father, grant that every man will execute judgment and show mercy and compassions to his/her brother/sister in Jesus name. 7 vs. 9
6. Father keep the widows free from oppression in Jesus name
7. May we not imagine evil against our brother/sister in Jesus name 7 vs. 10
8. Father may my seed be prosperous in Jesus name
9. May my vine give her fruit in Jesus name
10. May my ground give her increase in Jesus name
11. May the heavens give its dew in Jesus name
12. May I possess my possession in Jesus name 8 vs. 12
13. Sanctify me Lord in the truth that I may speak the truth to my neighbor in Jesus name 8 vs. 16
14. May I not imagine evil in my heart in Jesus name

15. May I not love false oath in Jesus name
16. May I not do things that you hate Lord 8 vs. 17
17. Father, cut off the pride of my enemies in Jesus name 9 vs. 6
18. Father, encamp round about your children, let no oppressor come near us in Jesus name 9 vs. 8
19. Father, cut off the powers of my enemies in Jesus name 9 vs. 10

Malachi

Prayer points:
1. Father I will not rob you in Jesus name
2. May I have the desire and commitment to pay my tithe when due in Jesus name
3. Father, open the windows of heaven and pour out a blessing that there will be no room enough to receive it in Jesus name
4. Father rebuke the devourer for my sake in Jesus name
5. May the enemy not destroy my ground in Jesus name
6. May my vine not cast her fruit before the time in the field in Jesus name
7. May all nations call me blessed in Jesus name
8. Make me a delightsome land in Jesus name
9. Father, may I not be burned like the wicked as a stubble
10. Father, may the sun of righteousness arise upon me and my family in Jesus name
11. May the sun bring healing in his wings and heal me and my family in Jesus name
12. May I tread down the wicked in accordance to your word in Jesus name.
13. May the enemies be ashes under the soles of my feet in accordance to your word in Jesus name

New Testament

Prayer points from Mathew

1. Father, like Joseph, may I be a just woman/man who is not quick to put brethren to shame for their mistakes in Jesus name
2. Father, like Joseph, may I not spread what I think is the wrongdoing of a brethren in Jesus name.
3. Father, like Joseph, may I not be quick to make conclusions regarding brethren in Jesus name
4. May I take my time, like Joseph to ponder things in my heart and commit issues to God in prayer in Jesus name.
5. Father may your angels appear to me in my dreams constantly and speak to me regarding any issue or decision that I need to take in Jesus name.
6. Father, may I be obedient to your word as your angel will minister it to me in Jesus name. Matt. 1
7. Father, give me the grace to fast forty days and forty nights as our Lord Jesus did in Jesus name.
8. Father prepare me at all times to defeat the tempter in Jesus name.
9. Father, may I study your word, and know your word so that I can defeat the enemy with your word in Jesus name. Matt. 4
10. Father, may I not be angry with my brethren without a cause in Jesus name
11. May I not be in danger of judgment in Jesus name. Matt. 5 vs. 22
12. Father give me the grace to love my enemies in Jesus name
13. Father give me the grace not to curse my enemies in Jesus name
14. Father give me the grace to bless my enemies in Jesus name
15. Father give me the grace to do good to my enemies in Jesus name.

16. Father give me the grace to pray for those who despitefully use and persecute me in Jesus name. Matt 5 vs. 44

17. I pray God that when I ask I will receive in Jesus name

18. I pray that when I seek, I will find in accordance to your word

19. I pray that when I knock, the door shall be opened unto me in Jesus name. Matt 7 vs 7.

20. Father, I pray for your power to come over/upon me that I can heal the sick in accordance to your word.

21. Give me the power Lord to cleanse lepers in Jesus name

22. Give me the anointing/power to raise the dead and cast out devils in Jesus name. Matt 10 vs. 8.

23. Father, your word says that all men for your name's sake shall hate me, but he that endures to the end shall be saved. Lord I pray to be baptized with the spirit of endurance that I may endure to the end and be saved in Jesus name Matt. 10 vs. 22.

24. Father, I come to you with my labor

25. Father, I come to you with my heavy burden

26. Father I come to you to receive rest

27. Give me rest Lord in Jesus name. Matt 11 vs. 28

28. Father, give me the command that will heal me

29. Give me the command that will deliver me

30. Give me the command that will set me free

31. May I be obedient to your commandments in Jesus name. Matt 12 vs. 13

32. Father, reveal the plan of the enemy against me to me.

33. Give me wisdom to withdraw myself from the attack of my enemies in Jesus name. Matt 12 vs. 14

34. Father, set a watch over my mouth in Jesus name.

35. Father, when I speak, may my words not be idle words in Jesus name.

36. May the words of my mouth not condemn me in Jesus name. Matt 12 vs. 36 & 37.

37. May I continuously honor my father and mother

38. May I not curse my father or mother in Jesus name. Matt. 15 vs. 4.

39. May every plant that God has not planted in me be rooted out in Jesus name. vs. 13.
40. May evil not proceed out of my heart in Jesus name
41. May the thought of murder not proceed out of my heart in Jesus name.
42. May the thought of evil not proceed out of my heart in Jesus name.
43. May I not think of adultery in Jesus name.
44. May I not think of fornication in Jesus name
45. May I not think of being a false witness that I may not be defiled in Jesus name. Matt. 15 vs. 19
46. Father, your word commanded that whatever we bind on earth shall be bound in heaven and whatever we loose on earth shall be loosed in heaven. Therefore, you spirit of war I bind you and I release the spirit of peace in Jesus name
47. Sprit of poverty I bind you and release the spirit of the power to make wealth in Jesus name
48. Spirit of sickness I bind you and I release the spirit of healing in Jesus name
49. Spirit of disease I bind you and release spirit of divine perfect health in Jesus name
50. Spirit of lie I bind you and release spirit of truth in Jesus name
51. Spirit of hatred I bind you and release spirit of love in Jesus name
52. Spirit of divorce I bind you and release spirit of 'till death do us part' in Jesus name. Matt. 16 vs. 19.
53. May I have the faith as little as a mustard seed in Jesus name
54. May I have the faith that can move mountains in Jesus name
55. May I have the faith that can make nothing impossible for me in Jesus name. Matt 17 vs. 20
56. May I humble myself as a little child in Jesus name. Matt. 18 vs. 4
57. Give me the grace to tell my brother/sister his/her fault against me in Jesus name. Matt. 18 vs. 15

58. Father, I pray for the grace to forgive anyone that has offended me in Jesus name. Matt. 18 vs. 35

59. Father, may there be cleaving of a husband to his wife in accordance to your word among brethren, that the two shall be one flesh in Jesus name.

60. Father may the enemy not be able to put asunder what you have joined together in Jesus name. Matt. 19 vs. 5 & 6

61. Father grant me the grace to keep your commandments that I may enter into life in accordance to your word in Jesus name. vs. 17b

62. Father, may the kingdom of God not be taken from me for being fruitless in Jesus name.

63. Father, I will bear fruit that will abide in Jesus name. Matt. 21 vs. 43

64. Father, may I not err not knowing the scripture or the power of God. Matt. 22 vs. 29

65. Father, may I love you with all my heart in Jesus name

66. Father, may I love you with all my soul in Jesus name

67. Father, may I love you with all my mind in Jesus name

68. Father, may I love my neighbor as myself in Jesus name. vs. 37 & 39

69. Spirit of deception I come against you in Jesus name

70. I will not be deceived in Jesus name.

71. I will take heed in Jesus name. Matt. 24 vs. 4

72. Father, may I not serve you in vain in Jesus name

73. May I endure to the end so that I will be saved in Jesus name. vs. 13

74. May all the blessings that you have spoken concerning me come to pass in my life in Jesus name. vs. 35

75. Holy Spirit, help me to watch that I may not miss the hour of the coming of our Lord Jesus in Jesus name. vs. 42

76. Father, I pray that I will be able to stay in your presence at least one hour in a day in Jesus name.

77. Help me Holy Spirit to watch and pray that I may not enter into temptation in Jesus name.

78. May my spirit be stronger than my flesh in Jesus name. Matt. 26 vs.40b & 41

79. Father, send your angel from heaven to roll away all my problems as the angel rolled back the stone from the door of the tomb where Jesus was laid in Jesus name

80. Father, send your angel to roll back all the hindrances before me and sit upon them that I may be set free in Jesus name. Matt. 28 vs. 2

81. Holy Spirit, help me to obey God's word in Jesus name

82. Help me Holy Spirit to go in the name of the Father, Son and Holy Spirit and teach all the nations and baptize them in Jesus name. vs. 19 & 20

Prayer points from Mark

1. Father, may your spirit have absolute control of my life and drive me wherever you want Lord in Jesus name. Mk.1 vs. 12

2. Lord Jesus, calm the raging storm in my home in Jesus name

3. Arise Jesus and rebuke the evil wind that is blowing in my home in Jesus name

4. Speak peace to my life in Jesus name.

5. Speak peace to my marriage in Jesus name

6. Speak peace to everything that concerns me in Jesus name

7. Let the trouble in my marriage cease in Jesus name

8. Let the trouble in my home cease in Jesus name

9. Let the trouble in my family cease in Jesus name

10. Let there be a great calm all around me in Jesus name Mk. 4 vs. 39

11. Father, cast out all the devils tormenting me in Jesus name

12. Father, cast out all the devils tormenting my home in Jesus name

13. Father, cast out all the devils tormenting my husband/wife in Jesus name

14. Father, cast out all the devils tormenting my children in Jesus name

15. Father, cast out all the devils tormenting my marriage in Jesus name
16. I anoint myself for healing in Jesus name
17. I anoint my home for healing in Jesus name
18. I anoint my husband/wife for healing in Jesus name
19. I anoint my children for healing in Jesus name
20. I anoint my sick marriage for healing in Jesus name. Mk. 6 vs. 13
21. Father, I believe, make all things possible for me in Jesus name
22. Father, forgive my unbelief in Jesus name. Mk. 9 vs. 23 & 24

Prayer Points from Luke

1. Father may my spouse and I be righteous before you in Jesus name
2. May we walk in all your commandments and ordinances in Jesus name
3. May we live a blameless life in Jesus name. Lk. 1 vs. 6
4. Father, I believe your promises concerning me in Jesus name
5. Father, let there be a performance of your words concerning me in Jesus name. vs. 45
6. Father, save my family and I from our enemies in Jesus name
7. Father, save my family and I from the hand of all that hate us in Jesus name. vs. 71
8. Father, fill every valley in my life in Jesus name
9. Every mountain and hill in my life, I command you to be brought down in Jesus name.
10. Father, let every crooked thing in my life be made straight in Jesus name
11. Father, every rough way that I am going through now, be made smooth in Jesus name. Lk. 3 vs. 5
12. Father in Lk. 4, the devil did not give up, therefore I will not give up in Jesus name

13. Father, may I live a holy and righteous life that my words will proceed with power in Jesus name. vs. 32.
14. Father, speak your word into my life in Jesus name
15. Father, speak your word into my circumstance in Jesus name
16. Father, speak your word into my situation in Jesus name. Lk. 5 vs. 5b
17. Like our Lord Jesus, may my desire be to pray and may I pray all night in Jesus name
18. Father, may I consult and hear from you before making any decision big or small in Jesus name.
19. Father, forgive all the times that I have made decisions without committing them into your hand and waiting to hear from you in Jesus name. Lk. 6 vs. 12 & 13
20. Father, I pray that I will go throughout the world preaching and sharing the glad tidings of the kingdom of God in Jesus name. Lk. 8 vs. 1
21. Father, I pray that I will hear your word and keep your word in Jesus name. Lk. 11 vs. 28
22. Father, baptize me with the fire of prayer in Jesus name
23. May I always pray and not faint in Jesus name Lk. 18 vs. 1
24. Father, because I trouble you, avenge me of my enemies in Jesus name
25. Father, avenge me of my enemies speedily in Jesus name. vs. 5 – 8
26. Father, send your angel from heaven to strengthen me in Jesus name. Lk. 22 vs. 43

Prayer Points from St. John

1. Father I commit into your hands my friends and family members (name them) that do not know you yet, I pray for the salvation of their souls in Jesus name.
2. I pray Lord that I will be able to see the kingdom of God in Jesus name

3. Every veil that is blocking my parents, siblings, husband/wife, children and friends from seeing the danger that they are in, Father remove them in Jesus name

4. Father, your word says that except a man be born again he cannot see the kingdom of God, Father, I want to see the kingdom of God. I want my children to see the kingdom of God, I want my husband/wife to see the kingdom of God, I want my siblings to see the kingdom of God, I want my friends to see the kingdom of God, I want my neighbors to see the kingdom of God in Jesus name. Jn. 3 vs. 3.

5. Father, I want to be born of water and of the spirit that I may enter into the kingdom of God in Jesus name. vs. 5

6. Father I pray to continue to believe in the Son of God so that I will not perish but have eternal life in Christ Jesus in Jesus name.

7. Father, baptize me with the spirit of love, that I may minister your word in Jesus name. vs. 16

8. Father, I confess that I believe in the Son, I confess that I have everlasting life in Jesus name.

9. I refuse to see the wrath of God in Jesus name

10. I will see life in Jesus name. vs. 36.

11. Father God, I will lift you up in all I do that all men may be drawn unto you in Jesus name. 12 vs. 32

12. Holy Spirit help me to keep the commandments of Christ in Jesus name.

13. Jesus, pray the Father to give me another Comforter that will abide with me forever in Jesus name

14. Lord Jesus send your spirit of truth to be with me in Jesus name

15. Father, may I know the spirit of truth.

16. Father, may I receive the spirit of truth in Jesus name

17. Lord Jesus, please do not leave me comfortless in Jesus name

18. Holy Spirit help me to keep Christ's commands so that He will manifest himself to me in Jesus name.

19. My heart will not be troubled in Jesus name.

20. Father, may I be a branch that bears fruit so that I will not be plucked away, but be purged that I may bring forth more fruit in Jesus name. 15 vs. 2

21. I receive you Lord Jesus fully into my heart, that I may be able to do everything in accordance to your word. Vs. 5b

22. Father, I pray to abide in Christ the vine and that Christ abide in me in Jesus name that I shall ask what I will and it shall be done unto me in Jesus name. vs. 7

23. Father, I pray that I will love my brethren in accordance to your word for my joy to be full in Jesus name.

24. Father, may the spirit of truth abide in me, may the spirit show me things to come in Jesus name. 16 vs. 13b

25. Father, in accordance to your word, may I receive whatever I ask in the name of Jesus in accordance to your will for my life. Vs. 23

26. Father, may I have peace continually in you in Jesus name vs. 33

27. Father, in accordance to your word, sanctify me through thine truth, for your word is truth. 17 vs. 17

28. Father, I pray that I will speak your word to others and they will believe and be partakers of the prayer that Christ prays for the church in Jesus name

29. My sorrow is finished in Jesus name

30. My disappointments are over in Jesus name

31. Failure is over in Jesus name

32. Sadness is over in Jesus name

33. My dreams will come to pass in Jesus name

34. God let every of my vision come to reality in accordance to your will for my life in Jesus name 19 vs. 30

35. I receive the Holy Ghost in Jesus name

36. I receive the power to forgive sin in Jesus name. 20 vs. 22b &23

Prayer Points from Acts

1. I receive the power of the Holy Ghost in Jesus name
2. May I be a witness unto you Lord Jesus in the name of Jesus 1 vs. 8
3. Father, pour your spirit upon all flesh in accordance to your word
4. May our sons and daughters prophesy in Jesus name
5. May our young men see visions in the name of Jesus
6. May our old men dream dreams in Jesus name 2 vs. 17
7. May whoever call on your name be saved in accordance to your word in Jesus name.
8. May we be saved from childbearing in Jesus name
9. Father, may we be saved from the evil plans of our enemies in Jesus name
10. Father, may we be saved from the trap that the enemy has set for us in Jesus name
11. Father, may we be saved from the pit that the enemy has dug for us in Jesus name vs. 21
12. Lord Jesus because you are on my right hand, I cannot be moved vs. 25b
13. My heart will rejoice and my tongue glad in Jesus name vs. 26
14. Father, I pray that my attitude wherever I go will reflect Christ in me in Jesus name 4 vs. 13
15. Lord make me bold in all things, bold to speak your word in Jesus name. vs. 19
16. Father, fill me with the Holy Spirit that I may speak the word of God with boldness in Jesus name vs. 31
17. Father, may your children be of one accord in Jesus name. 5 vs. 12b
18. Father, may I choose to obey you rather than men in Jesus name vs. 29
19. Father, be with me at all times and everywhere even in Egypt in Jesus name 7 vs. 9
20. Father, deliver me from all my afflictions in Jesus name

21. Father give me favor in Jesus name
22. Father give me wisdom in the sight of all including my enemies.
23. May I be promoted in all that I do in Jesus name
24. May I be head and not tail in Jesus name vs. 10
25. Father, hear my affliction, hear my groaning and come down and deliver me in Jesus name. vs. 34
26. Father, send me to the needy in Jesus name vs. 34b
27. Father, may I fear you that you may accept me in accordance to your word. 10 vs. 35
28. Father, may we learn as a church to make prayer for one another concerning our needs without ceasing in Jesus name 12 vs. 5b
29. Father, may I be a light unto sinners in Jesus name
30. Father may I be for salvation unto the ends of the earth in Jesus name 13 vs. 47
31. Father grant that I shall speak your words in season and out of season and may it be accompanied with signs and wonders in Jesus name. 14.
32. Father, give me the grace and boldness to minister your word in Jesus name
33. Father, give me the grace to follow up with as many as I minister your word to in Jesus name 15 vs. 36
34. Father, I pray that as I begin to pray and sing unto you at my midnight, that there will be great earthquake, so that the foundation of my problem will be shaken in Jesus name
35. Father, open all my closed doors and cause every bonds to loose in Jesus name 16 vs. 25 & 26
36. Father, may I receive the word with all readiness of mind
37. Father, may I search the scriptures daily to see whether what I have heard is as spoken in Jesus name 17 vs. 11
38. Father, may I continue to live, move and have my being in you in Jesus name vs. 28
39. Father, may I be holy enough for you to speak to me in a vision of the night in Jesus name

40. Father may I remember everything that you will speak to me in Jesus name

41. Father, may I be obedient to your words in Jesus name

42. Father, may I not be afraid to speak your word in Jesus name

43. Father, be with me, that no man shall hurt me in Jesus name. 18 vs. 9 & 10

44. Father, wrought special miracles by my hand in Jesus name.

45. Father, give me power to heal diseases in Jesus name.

46. Father, give me power to cast out evil spirits in Jesus name 19 vs. 11 & 12

47. Father, may I not count my life dear unto myself, so that I might finish my course with joy and the ministry, which I have received of the Lord Jesus, to testify the gospel of the grace of God.

48. Father, may I not be moved by the troubles of this world in Jesus name 10 vs. 22

49. Father, the expectation of my enemies concerning me will not come to pass in Jesus name.

50. My enemies will look expecting harm to come to me, but they will see no harm come to me in Jesus name.

51. My enemies will change their mind concerning me in Jesus name. 28 vs. 6b

Prayer Points from Romans

1. I will not be ashamed of the gospel of Christ in Jesus name

2. The gospel of Christ is the power of God unto salvation to everyone that believe 1 vs. 16

3. I will live by faith in Jesus name vs. 17. John 3: 36 says that he that believes in the Son has everlasting life, and he that does not believe in the Son shall not see life but wrath of God abide on him

4. Father, may your goodness lead my friends and family members that are not safe to repentance in Jesus name. 2 vs. 4

5. May glory, honor, and peace follow me even as I work in Jesus name. vs. 10
6. Father, your word says that whosoever believeth in Christ shall not be ashamed, I shall not be ashamed in Jesus name 9 vs. 33.
7. Father, may I abhor that which is evil and cleave to that which is good in Jesus name 12 vs. 9
8. May I not be slothful in business in Jesus name
9. May I be fervent in spirit in Jesus name
10. May I serve the Lord in Jesus name
11. May I rejoice in hope in Jesus name
12. May I be patient in tribulation in Jesus name
13. May I continue constant in prayer in Jesus name
14. May I distribute to the necessity of saints in Jesus name
15. May I give to hospitality in Jesus name
16. May I bless them which persecute me in Jesus name
17. May I not curse in Jesus name
18. May I rejoice with them that rejoice in Jesus name
19. May I weep with them that weep in Jesus name vs. 10 – 15
20. Lord Jesus, help me to live peaceably with all men.
21. Father, take vengeance on my enemies
22. May I not avenge myself in Jesus name vs.18 & 19
23. May I not be overcome of evil but overcome evil with good in Jesus name. vs.21
24. Father, I pray to put on the Lord Jesus Christ fully that I may not make provision for flesh to fulfill the lusts thereof in Jesus name 13 vs. 14
25. Every problem that I am passing through right now bow in Jesus name
26. May every mouth confess that you are Lord, Lord Jesus in Jesus name 14 vs.11
27. Lord I pray for a constant desire to pray for church leaders in Jesus name.
28. I pray that my pastors be delivered from unbelievers in Jesus name.

29. I pray that my pastors will fulfill their ministry in Jesus name 15 vs. 30 & 31

Prayer Points from First Corinthians

1. Father, may I not miss out on the things which you have prepared for me, that eyes had not seen, nor ear heard, neither have entered into the heart of man in Jesus name. 2 vs. 9
2. I am the temple of God, I will remain the temple of God in Jesus name
3. The Spirit of God dwells in me
4. The Spirit of God will continue to dwell in me and not depart in Jesus name 3 vs. 16
5. Father deliver me from fornication in Jesus name
6. Father deliver me from idolatry in Jesus name
7. Father deliver me from adultery in Jesus name
8. Father deliver me from abusing mankind in Jesus name
9. Father deliver me from theft in Jesus name
10. Father deliver me from covetousness in Jesus name
11. Father deliver me from drunkenness in Jesus name
12. Father deliver me from reviling in Jesus name
13. Father deliver me from being an extortioner in Jesus name
14. Father may I inherit the kingdom of God in Jesus name 6 vs. 9b & 10
15. I will glorify God in my body in Jesus name
16. I will glorify God in my spirit in Jesus name vs. 20
17. Father your word said that he that ploweth should plow in hope, and that he that thresheth in hope should be partaker of his hope, therefore, Lord God, I am believing you for a turning around of situations in my life. Everything that has caused me to weep, I am believing will bring me joy, I receive them now in the name of Jesus 9 vs. 10b
18. Father may I not lust after evil things in Jesus name 10 vs. 6
19. I will not murmur in Jesus name vs. 10

20. I will not be tempted above that which I can bear in Jesus name.
21. Father, with every temptation you will make a way of escape for me in Jesus name vs. 13
22. Father, may my mind be like that of a child in malice in Jesus name
23. May my mind be like that of a man in understanding in Jesus name 14 vs. 20
24. Father, may your grace which is bestowed upon me not be in vain in Jesus name 15 vs. 10
25. Father, give me victory over my enemies through Jesus Christ in Jesus name vs. 57.
26. Father may I be steadfast, unmovable, always abounding in the work of the Lord in Jesus name
27. Father, may my labor not be in vain in Jesus name vs. 58
28. Father, give me the grace to watch, stand fast in faith and quit like a man and be strong in the Lord in Jesus name
29. Father may I do all things with love in Jesus name 16 vs. 13 & 14

Prayer Points from Second Corinthians

1. Blessed be God, even the Father of our Lord Jesus Christ, the Father of mercies, and God of all comfort
2. Blessed be God who comfort us in all our tribulation, that we may be able to comfort them which are in any trouble, by the comfort wherewith we ourselves are comforted of God 1 vs. 3 - 4
3. Father, let your spirit come into my home, that there may be liberty in my home in Jesus name
4. Father, send your spirit into my marriage, that there may be liberty in Jesus name
5. Father, send your spirit into the body of Christ your church that there may be liberty

6. Father send your spirit into my life that I will live in liberty in Jesus name 3 vs. 17
7. May I not be unequally yoked with an unbeliever in Jesus name 6 vs. 14
8. Father, in sowing may I not sow sparingly in Jesus name
9. Father, in reaping, may I not reap sparingly in Jesus name 9 vs. 6
10. Father, may I not give grudgingly in Jesus name vs. 7

Prayer Points from Galatians

1. Father may I not confer with flesh and blood before doing your will in Jesus name 1 vs. 16
2. Father reveal to me your calling for my life in Jesus name 2 vs. 7
3. I confess that I am crucified with Christ, nevertheless I live, yet not I, but Christ lives in me and the life that I live in the flesh I live by the faith of the Son of God, who loved me and gave himself for me vs. 20
4. Father, may I be a just person that I may live by faith in Jesus name 3 vs. 11b
5. Father, let he that troubles me bear his judgment, whosoever he be in Jesus name 5 vs. 10b
6. Father, cut off they which trouble me in Jesus name vs. 12
7. Father, may I work in the Spirit at all times that I may not fulfill the lust of the flesh in Jesus name vs. 16
8. Father may I not be desirous of vain glory in Jesus name
9. Father may I not provoke my brethren in Jesus name
10. Father may I not envy my brethren in Jesus name vs. 26
11. Father may I not sow to the flesh in Jesus name
12. Father may I sow to the Spirit that I may reap everlasting life in Jesus name
13. Father may I not be weary in well doing in Jesus name
14. May I not faint in well doing that I may reap in due season in Jesus name

15. As often as I have the opportunity, Lord grant I will use it to do good unto all men in Jesus name 6 vs. 8 – 10

16. Let no man trouble me for I bear in my body the marks of the Lord Jesus vs. 17

Prayer Points from Ephesians

1. Glory be unto you God who is able to do exceeding abundantly beyond our thoughts or imagination. 3 vs. 20

2. Father, when I am angry, may I not sin in Jesus name 4 vs. 26

3. Father, I pray that no corrupt communication will come out of my mouth in Jesus

4. Father I pray that only things that are good and used for edifying, that will minister grace to the hearers will proceed out of my mouth in Jesus name

5. I will not grieve the Holy Spirit of God, in whom I am sealed unto the day of redemption in Jesus name

6. Bitterness, wrath, anger, clamor, and evil speaking, I command you by the power that is in the blood to get of my spirit, soul, and body in Jesus name 4 vs.29 – 31

7. Father, I will give you thanks always for all things in Jesus name 5 vs. 20

8. Holy Spirit teach me to not provoke my children in Jesus name

9. Holy Spirit, teach me how to bring up my children in the nurture and admonition of the Lord in Jesus name 6 vs. 4

10. Holy Spirit teach me to pray always with all prayer and supplication in the Spirit in Jesus name

11. Holy Spirit teach me to watch with all perseverance and supplication for all saints in Jesus name

12. Holy Spirit teach me to pray for ministers and children of God that utterance will be given unto them, that they may open their mouths boldly to make known the mystery of the gospel in Jesus name vs. 18 – 19

Prayer Points from Philippians

1. Lord Jesus, you that began a good work in me, will perform it till the end in Jesus name 1 v. 6

2. Father may I work out my salvation with fear and trembling in Jesus name. 2 v. 12b

3. May I do all things without murmurings and disputing in Jesus name

4. May I be a blameless and harmless child of God in the midst of a crooked and perverse nation.

5. May I shine as light in the world in Jesus name vs. 14 – 15

6. Lord Jesus, I want to know you and the power of your resurrection in Jesus name 3 v.10

7. Father, give me the grace to press toward the mark for the prize of the high calling of God in Christ Jesus in Jesus name v.14

8. Father, may I rejoice in you always in Jesus name. 4 v. 4

9. May I in everything by prayer and supplication, with thanksgiving let my request be made known unto you Father God in Jesus name

10. May the peace of God, which passes all understanding, keep my heart and mind through Christ Jesus.

11. May I speak whatever is true in Jesus name

12. May I speak and do whatever is honest in Jesus name

13. May I speak and do whatever is pure, lovely, and of good report in Jesus name.

14. If there be any virtue, and if there be any praise, may I think on such things in Jesus name. v. 8

15. Father, in accordance to your word, I confess that I can do all things through Christ who strengthens me in Jesus name v. 13

16. I confess with my mouth that my God shall supply all my needs according to his riches in glory by Christ Jesus v. 19

Prayer Points from Colossians

1. Father may I walk in Christ all the days of my life in Jesus name
2. Father may I teach my children to walk in Christ all the days of their lives in Jesus name
3. May I be rooted and built up in Christ in Jesus name
4. May I be established in faith in Jesus Christ.
5. May I abound and abide in Christ in Jesus name 2 vs. 6 & 7
6. Thank you Lord Jesus for blotting out the handwriting of ordinances that were against me, which were contrary to me in Jesus name
7. Thank you Lord Jesus for nailing the ordinances and the handwriting against me to the cross in Jesus name
8. Thank you, for spoiling principalities and powers in Jesus nane
9. Thank you, for making a show of them openly, and triumphing over them in Jesus name vs. 14 & 15
10. Holy Spirit, help me to set my affections on things that are above, not on things on earth in Jesus name.
11. May my life be continuously hid in Christ Jesus in Jesus name 3 vs. 2 & 3
12. Holy Spirit, help me to put off anger, wrath, malice, blasphemy, filthy communication out of my mouth in Jesus name
13. Spirit of lies, I come against you in Jesus name, for I have put off the old man with his deeds and I have put on the new man, the spirit of truth in Jesus name vs. 8 – 10
14. As the beloved of God, I put on mercy, kindness, humility, meekness, longsuffering, and spirit of forgiveness in Jesus name vs. 12 - 13
15. Father, may the word of Christ dwell in me richly in all wisdom in Jesus name. v. 16
16. May I do everything out of a pure heart as to the Lord and not unto men in Jesus name v. 23

17. May my speech be always with grace, seasoned with salt, that I may know how I am supposed to answer every man in Jesus name 4 v. 6

Prayer Points from First Thessalonians

1. Father, make me to increase and abound in love toward my brethren and all men in Jesus name 3 v. 12
2. Father may I learn to be quiet and to do my own business and to work with my own hands in Jesus name
3. May I walk honestly in Jesus name
4. Father may I have lack of nothing in Jesus name 4 vs. 11 – 12
5. Father, may I not miss the day of the Lord that cometh as a thief in the night
6. May I be ready for the coming of our Lord Jesus in Jesus name 5 v. 2
7. I will not sleep, I will watch and be sober in Jesus name v. 6
8. I will be at peace with my brethren in Jesus name
9. I will rejoice evermore in Jesus name
10. I will pray without ceasing in Jesus name
11. I will give thanks to God in everything for I know it is the will of God in Christ Jesus concerning me
12. I will not quench the Spirit in Jesus name
13. I will not despise prophesying in Jesus name
14. I will hold fast unto that which is good in Jesus name
15. I will abstain from all appearance of evil in Jesus name
16. May the God of peace sanctify me holy in Jesus name
17. May my whole spirit be preserved blameless unto the coming of our Lord Jesus Christ. Vs. 16 – 23

Prayer Points from Second Thessalonians

1. May I not be weary in well doing in Jesus name

Prayer Points from First Timothy

1. Glory be unto the king eternal, immortal, invisible, the only wise God. in Jesus name 1 v. 17
2. Father, may I make supplications, prayers, intercession and giving of thanks for all men in Jesus name
3. Father, may I take time out of my schedule everyday to pray for the president of my country and for those in authority, that we may lead a quiet and peaceable life in all godliness and honesty
4. Father, may I take time out of my schedule to pray for all the heads of households, that the family will live a peaceable, quiet life in all godliness and honesty in Jesus name 2 vs. 1 & 2
5. Father, may I live an exemplary Christian life in Jesus name 4 v. 12

Prayer Points from Second Timothy

1. God I receive your word that says that you have not given me the spirit of fear in Jesus name
2. I receive the spirit of power in Jesus name
3. I receive spirit of love and soundness of mind in Jesus name 1v. 7
4. Holy Spirit, my teacher, help me to study the word of God to show myself approved unto God, a workman that need not be ashamed, rightly dividing the word of truth in Jesus name 2 v. 15
5. Holy Spirit, teach me to shun profane and vain babblings, that increase unto more ungodliness in Jesus name v. 16
6. Father, as I confess and minister the word of the Lord, may the Holy Spirit lead me in the path that departs from iniquity in Jesus name v. 19

7. Holy Spirit, help me to flee youthful lust, but to follow righteousness, faith, charity, peace, with them that call on the Lord out of a pure heart in Jesus name v. 22

8. Holy Spirit, help me not to strive, but to be gentle unto all men and teach in patience in Jesus name v. 24

9. May I in meekness, instruct those that oppose themselves in Jesus name v. 25

10. Holy Spirit, help me to preach the word, be instant in season, out of season, reprove, rebuke, exhort with all longsuffering and doctrine in Jesus name 4 v. 2

11. Father, like Paul, may I be able to say that I have fought the good fight, I have finished my course, I have kept the faith. Henceforth there is laid up for me a crown of righteousness, which the Lord, the righteous judge, shall give me at that day in Jesus name v. 8

Prayer Points from Titus

1. Holy Spirit, take control of my mouth that I may speak evil of no man in Jesus name

2. Spirit of gentleness come upon me now and overshadow me in Jesus name

3. Spirit of meekness come upon me now in Jesus name 3 v. 2

Prayer Points from Philemon

1. I receive grace to pray for brethren

2. Father, I pray for increased faith among brethren

3. Father, I pray for love among brethren

4. Father, I pray that we will be profitable to one another

5. I pray that we will receive one another with love

6. I pray that we will see ourselves as equal before you oh Lord

7. I pray that in whatever gathering of believers we find ourselves that we will feel at home

8. I pray that we will make other believers who come into our midst to feel at home in Jesus name

Prayer Points from Hebrews

1. Father, give me the grace to call on brethren to exhort them daily, while it is called today, lest any of us be hardened through the deceitfulness of sin in Jesus name 3 v. 13
2. Father let your word that is quick and powerful, and sharper that any two-edged sword pierce the heart of my husband/ wife and deliver him/her in Jesus name (Put the name of any friend or family member that you have been praying for the salvation of their soul there) 4 v. 12
3. Father, in blessing, bless me, in multiplying multiply me in Jesus name 6 v. 14
4. Father, let your laws be put in my mind, be written in my heart and be to me a God and may I continually be your child in Jesus name 8 v. 10
5. Father, may I hold fast the profession of my faith without wavering because I know that you God that has promised to deliver me on the day of trouble will fulfill your promise in my life in Jesus name. 10 v. 23
6. Father, may I not forsake the assembly of brethren in Jesus name v. 25
7. Father, take vengeance on my enemies in Jesus name
8. Holy Spirit, help me not to cast away my confidence in Jesus name v. 35
9. Father, may I not draw back, that you may have confidence in me in Jesus name v. 38
10. Father, may I run with patience the race that is set before me in Jesus name 12 v. 1
11. Father, may I look unto Jesus the author and finisher of my faith in Jesus name v. 2
12. Holy Spirit help me to follow peace with all men and to live a holy life in Jesus name v.14

13. Father, let your fire consume every evil and wickedness of the enemy around me in Jesus name v. 29

14. Father, I receive your word that says that you will never leave me nor forsake me in Jesus name 13 v. 5b

15. Father, I will confess with my mouth that the Lord is my helper, and I will not fear what man shall do unto me in Jesus name v. 6

16. Holy Spirit, help me to offer the sacrifice of praise to God continually, the fruit of my lips giving thanks to the name of the Almighty God in Jesus name v. 15

17. Holy Spirit, help me not to forget to do good in Jesus name v. 16

Prayer Points from James

1. Father God, I thank you for all the temptations that I have fallen into and for your deliverance in Jesus name 1 v. 2

2. Father, may the trying of my faith work patience in Jesus name v. 3

3. Give me wisdom Lord, for your word says that if I lack wisdom that I should ask God that gives to all men liberally, and upbraided not in Jesus name v. 5

4. Every spirit of doubt I come against you in Jesus name. I confess that I have faith and I shall have what I confess, I will not waver in Jesus name v.6

5. Father, thank you for the situation that I am passing through at this time, because I know that you will bring me to an expected end and I will not be put to shame in Jesus name v. 9

6. Holy Spirit, help me to endure all temptation in Jesus name.

7. May I receive the crown of life which Jesus promised to them that love him after being tried in Jesus name v. 12

8. Father, may I be swift to hear in Jesus name

9. Holy Spirit, put a watch over my mouth that I may be slow to speak in Jesus name

10. Holy Spirit, help me to be slow to wrath in Jesus name v. 19

11. Father may I not be hearer of your word only but a doer also in Jesus name v. 22
12. God stop the way of the proud and give grace to your humble children in Jesus name 4 v. 6
13. Father, I submit myself to you in Jesus name
14. Devil I resist you by the power in the blood of Jesus in Jesus name v. 7
15. Father, I humble myself before you that you may lift me up in Jesus name v. 10
16. Father, may I not speak evil of any brethren to another in Jesus name v. 11
17. I will not swear in Jesus name 5 v. 12
18. Father, I am afflicted, I pray God that you will deliver me from my affliction in Jesus name. v. 13
19. Father, I am sick, I pray that you heal me in Jesus name. v. 14
20. Father, forgive me my sins and heal me, deliver me in Jesus name v. 15

Prayer Points from First Peter

1. Holy Spirit, help me to be holy as he that has called me is holy in Jesus name 1 v. 15
2. Thank you Lord for choosing me in Jesus name
3. Thank you Lord for making me a royal priesthood in Jesus name
4. Thank you Lord for making me a peculiar person in Jesus name
5. Thank you Lord for calling me out of darkness into your marvelous light 2 v. 9
6. Holy Spirit help me to abstain from fleshly lust that war against the soul in Jesus name v. 11
7. May my conversations be honest even before my enemies that speak against me as evil doer in Jesus name v. 12
8. Holy Spirit help when I am reviled, not to revile again, and as I go through any suffering, let me not threaten any, but

commit myself to him that judge righteously in Jesus name v. 23

9. Thank you Lord Jesus Christ for your stripe by which I am healed in Jesus name v. 24b

10. Father, may I not render evil for evil in Jesus name 3 v. 9

11. May I not render railing for railing, but rather bless in Jesus name v. 9

12. Holy Spirit help me to remember that I have been called always, that I have been called that I should inherit a blessing in Jesus name v.9

13. Holy Spirit help me to refrain my tongue from evil and my lips that they speak no guile that I may have life and see good days in Jesus name v.10

14. Holy Spirit help me to eschew evil, to do good, to seek peace in Jesus name v. 11

15. Thank you Lord for your word that says your eyes are over me and your ears are open unto my prayers, hear my prayers therefore and deliver me and my family from the oppression of the enemy in Jesus name v. 12

16. Father, let your face be against my enemies in Jesus name. v. 12

17. There is no one that can harm me because I am a follower of Christ the Lord in Jesus name v. 13

18. I will not be afraid of the terror of my enemies in Jesus name v. 14

19. Holy Spirit, help me to sanctify the Lord at all times in my heart, teach me to be ready always to give answer to every man that ask me the reason of my hope that is Christ with meekness and fear in Jesus name. v. 15

20. Father, put to shame they that falsely accuse me and speak evil of me in Jesus name v. 16

21. Father, I rather suffer for well doing than for doing evil. Keep evil desire far away from me in Jesus name v. 17

22. Holy Spirit, help me to use hospitality with my brethren without grudging in Jesus name 4 v. 9

23. Lord I pray that whenever I speak, I shall speak as the oracle of the Lord in Jesus name v. 11

24. Help me Holy Spirit to minister according to the ability the Lord gives me in Jesus name v. 11

25. Father, may I not suffer as a murderer in Jesus name v. 15

26. Father, may I not suffer as a thief in Jesus name v. 15

27. Father, may I not suffer as an evil doer in Jesus name v. 15

28. Father, may I not suffer as a busy body in other men's matters in Jesus name v. 15

29. I come against the spirit of pride in Jesus name

30. I receive the spirit of grace in Jesus name 5 v. 5b

31. Holy Spirit, teach me to humble myself under the mighty hand of God, that he may exalt me in due time in Jesus name v. 6

32. Lord I cast all my care upon you for I know that you care for me in Jesus name v. 7

33. I will be sober, I will be vigilant, because my adversary the devil, as a roaring lion, walks about seeking whom he will devour v. 8

34. God, in accordance to your word, make me perfect, establish me, strengthen me and settle me in Jesus name v. 10

Prayer Points from Second Peter

1. Father, your word says that you know how to deliver the godly out of temptation, and to preserve the unjust unto the day of judgment to be punished. Lord in accordance to your word, deliver me in Jesus name 2 v. 9

2. Father, I know that you are not slack concerning your promise, deliver me Lord in Jesus name 3 v. 9

Prayer Points from First John

1. Father, I confess every one of my sins (name them). Forgive me Father because you a just God, you are a righteous God in Jesus name 1 v. 9

2. Holy Spirit, teach me to love my brethren, that I may abide in the light and let there be no occasion of stumbling in my life in Jesus name 2 v. 10

3. Holy Spirit, help me to keep your commandment and whatsoever I ask, may I receive in Jesus name 3 v. 22

4. Holy Spirit, teach me to continuously believe in the name of the Son of God Jesus Christ and to love the brethren as you command in Jesus name v. 23

5. Holy Spirit help me to keep the commandment of God that I may dwell in Him and He in me in Jesus name v. 24

6. Father, I confess in accordance to your word that greater is He that is in me than he that is in the world 4 v. 4b

7. Spirit of fear I come against you in Jesus name v. 18

8. I confess that I am born of God, therefore I can overcome the world in Jesus name

9. I confess that my faith in God will overcome the world and every plan of the enemy concerning me in Jesus name 5 v. 4

10. Father I have confidence that if I ask anything according to your will, you will hear and answer. Father in the name of Jesus, I ask for deliverance from the principalities and power, from spiritual wickedness in heavenly places in Jesus name v. 14

Prayer Points from Second John

1. Father, may I not lose my soul in Jesus name

2. May I gain the full reward of serving you in Jesus name 1 v. 8

Prayer Points from Third John

1. Father, I receive your word that says that you wish above all things that I prosper and be in health even as my soul prosper 1 v.2
2. I will prosper in Jesus name
3. I will be in health in Jesus name
4. I will not follow that which is evil in Jesus name
5. I will follow that which is good because I know God and God is good in Jesus name v. 11

Prayer Points from Jude

1. Father, may I not be a murmurer, and a complainer in Jesus name.
2. Father may I not walk lustfully and speak evil words in Jesus name 1 v. 16
3. Help me Holy Ghost to pray in Holy Ghost in Jesus name v. 20
4. Father may I hate the garment that is spotted by the flesh in Jesus name v. 23
5. You are the God that is able to keep me from falling, therefore I give you glory in Jesus name
6. Father, you are the only wise God, glory, honor and majesty, dominion and power be unto you now and forever in Jesus name v. 25

Prayer Points from Revelation

1. Lord I believe your word that you will come again in the clouds and every eye shall see you, and they that pierced you. Lord may I be found worthy when you come and may I rise to meet you in glory in Jesus name 1 v. 7
2. Lord I believe that you are the alpha and the omega, the beginning and the end. You are the Lord which is, which was and is to come, the Almighty v. 8

3. Holy Spirit help me to overcome that I may eat of the tree of life in Jesus name 2 v. 7b

4. Holy Spirit help me to be faithful unto the end that I may have the crown of life in Jesus name v.10

5. Holy Spirit, help me to overcome, that I may not be hurt by the second death in Jesus name v. 11

6. Holy Spirit, help me to watch that the coming of Christ will not be as a thief in the night to me in Jesus name 3 v. 3

7. Father your word says that you the God that opens and no man can shut, and shut and no man can open, shut every evil door of affliction in my life and open every door of victory in Jesus name v. 7

8. Father set before me continually an open door that no man can shut in Jesus name v. 8

9. Holy Spirit help me to hold fast unto that which I have that no man take my crown in Jesus name v. 11

10. Father, may I be hot for you that I will not be spewed out of your mouth God, in Jesus name v. 15

11. Father God, I invite you to come into my heart and sup with me all the time in Jesus name v. 20

12. I will not weep anymore because the Lion of the tribe of Judah, the root of David has prevailed in Jesus name 5 v. 5

13. Father, may I overcome the evil one by the blood of the Lamb, and by the word of my testimony in Jesus name 12 v. 11

14. Father, let the earth open and swallow the flood of the enemy in Jesus name v.16

15. Father, you are a great and marvelous God, you are the Almighty, just and true are your ways 15 v. 3b

16. Father, wipe away all tears from my eyes in Jesus name 21 v. 4

17. Take away the pains I am going through Lord, in Jesus name v.4

18. Holy Spirit help me to overcome that I may inherit all things and God will be my God in Jesus name v. 7

Benediction

Father in heaven, I thank you in the name of our Lord Jesus Christ for seeing me through the writing of this book, despite life's challenges. The challenges that you have seen me through, the ones you are seeing me through, and the ones that you will see me through, I thank you for all of them. Thank you Lord Jesus that neither principalities, power, depth nor height, spiritual wickedness in heavenly places were able to hinder the writing and publishing of this book. Father, to you be all the glory, honor, and adoration in Jesus name. Amen.

Appreciation

Back page picture was taken by my beloved brother Damola Onipede a humble man of God and an encourager. My Beloved Pastor Charlie Vincent, who feeds the sheep under his care with the SEED of the WORD. Yemi Kiyesi for reviewing and making corrections to the original manuscript. Thanks to my children Yemi and Wole for their support during the writing of this book. May you be richly blessed in Jesus name.

Printed in the United States
By Bookmasters